# CITYSPOTS
# HON

Helena Zukowski

**Written by Helena Zukowski**
Original photography by Helena Zukowski
Front cover photography © Travel Pix/Getty Images
Series design based on an original concept by Studio 183 Limited

**Produced by Cambridge Publishing Management Ltd**
Project Editor: Catherine Burch
Layout: Julie Crane
Maps: PC Graphics
Transport map: © Communicarta Ltd

**Published by Thomas Cook Publishing**
A division of Thomas Cook Tour Operations Limited
Company Registration No. 1450464 England
PO Box 227, Unit 18, Coningsby Road
Peterborough PE3 8SB, United Kingdom
email: books@thomascook.com
www.thomascookpublishing.com
+44 (0)1733 416477

**First edition © 2006 Thomas Cook Publishing**
Text © 2006 Thomas Cook Publishing
Maps © 2006 Thomas Cook Publishing
ISBN-13: 978-184157-632-9
ISBN-10: 1-84157-632-8
Series/Project Editor: Kelly Anne Pipes
Production/DTP: Steven Collins

Printed and bound in Spain by GraphyCems

# CONTENTS

## SYMBOLS & ABBREVIATIONS

The following symbols are used throughout this book:

ⓐ address   ☎ telephone   📠 fax   ✉ email   ⓦ website address
🕒 opening times   Ⓝ public transport connections   ❶ important

The following symbols are used on the maps:

| | | | |
|---|---|---|---|
| 𝒊 information office | | ○ city |
| ✈ airport | | ○ large town |
| ➕ hospital | | ○ small town |
| 🛡 police station | | ═ motorway |
| 🚌 bus station | | — main road |
| 🚆 railway station | | — minor road |
| Ⓜ metro | | — railway |
| ✝ cathedral | | |
| ❶ numbers denote featured cafés & restaurants | | |

Hotels and restaurants are graded by approximate price as follows:
£ budget   ££ mid-range   £££ expensive

◗ *Hong Kong's modern skyline*

# Introduction

At first sight, Hong Kong is like a huge pinball machine sitting by the sea – flashy, always on the move, all lights and action, a gambler's stab at the good life. It has been described to the point of cliché as a seamless blend of East and West, more modern than tomorrow but firmly anchored in ancient Chinese wisdom. Yet scratch below the surface and the cliché falls apart, for no other city frustrates the senses to such a degree or throws out such a bewildering set of contradictions.

Look around and you'll see the ultimate in modern architecture and technology beside run-down tenement buildings, age-old junks in the harbour next to sleek cruise ships. You can eat at restaurants that would out-class something in New York or slurp soup on the street at a *dai pai dong* (street cart). Despite Hong Kong now firmly being part of Communist China, the puzzling promise of 'one country, two systems' somehow seems to be finding its own level and the special blend of East and West totters on.

For those of us who have watched Hong Kong grow and change over many decades, the city never loses its fascination. The ride across 'fragrant harbour' (for this is what Hong Kong means) from Kowloon to Hong Kong Island on the Star Ferry will always be tinged with romance. The view from Victoria Peak will explain why Hong Kong is often called one of the five most beautifully set cities in the world. Most of all, despite the crowds, the pollution, the jostling and pushing, there is a profound admiration for a people who have the powerful capacity to persevere and endure. Since its birth, Hong Kong has been hit with setbacks galore, most recently from SARS, a massive economic depression, internal protests and external onslaughts on tourism because of 9/11.

In Chinese mythology the phoenix bird appears rarely but signals the birth of a new era. It hasn't been reported but in all likelihood a beautiful red bird is watching over Fragrant Harbour.

🔺 *The old and the new sit side by side in Hong Kong*

# When to go

### SEASONS & CLIMATE

Hong Kong is subtropical but still has its seasons. Spring (from March to mid-May) is warm but the humidity can be high and often fog and drizzle dampen the comfort level. Temperatures range from 18°C to 27°C (64–80°F) with an 82 per cent humidity. While days are warm, evenings can be cool enough for a lightweight jacket.

Summer (late May to mid-September) tends to be hot and humid with sweltering heat during mid-summer, so sightseeing can be a sweaty affair. This is also the rainy season, and warm but torrential downpours often quickly fill the streets. Temperatures range upwards from 33°C (91°F) with humidity near 86 per cent. Short sleeve cotton shirts are best, with a lightweight sweater to cope with heavily air-conditioned restaurants. Don't forget the umbrella – for rain or shine.

September brings a special problem – typhoons – and the threat seems to loom all month. From late September to early December the temperatures and humidity drop and days are clear and sunny; these are the best months to visit. Temperatures range from 18°C to 28°C (64–82°F) and the humidity is 72 per cent. Temperatures cool down in the winter (from mid-December to February) and nights can be quite chilly. It's a good idea to bring woollens and overcoats to cope with temperatures swings.

### ANNUAL EVENTS

Hong Kong is a city that loooooooooooves to celebrate, so you're likely to find something happening all year round. Since dates vary, it's a good idea to ask the HK Tourism website for a complete list if you want to hit the peak of the fun (www.discoverhongkong.com).

## January

During **Chinese New Year** (usually late January/early February), Hong Kong grinds to a virtual standstill for what is the most

⬥ *Traditional dragon dances greet the Chinese New Year*

important holiday of the Chinese year. Shops close for three days. There's a huge street parade on the first day, fireworks on the second and one of the largest horse races in Sha Tin on the third.

## February

Two of the month's best events are the **Hong Kong Arts Festival**, and the **Hong Kong Marathon**, attracting up to 30,000 participants. For more information check www.hk.artsfestival.org and www.hkmarathon.com

## March

The **Hong Kong Arts Festival** fills the city with four weeks of opera, jazz, classical music, theatre and dance performed by artists from around the globe. In late March/early April, The **Hong Kong Sevens** turns the city into 'rugby heaven' at the 40,000-seat Hong Kong Stadium.

### CHEUNG CHAU BUN FESTIVAL

Usually scheduled for the end of April/early May, the eight-day Cheung Chau Bun Festival honours the god Pak Tai whose 200-year-old temple is dedicated to the protection of fishermen. Three 20-m (66-ft) towers are covered with freshly baked sacred buns as an appeasement to the spirits of people killed by pirates. The climax traditionally came when people clambered up the towers to grab the highest buns (considered the most lucky) but after a tower collapsed some years ago the buns are now handed out. One of the festival's highlights is a parade where colourfully dressed children seem to float through the air, an illusion created by cleverly designed supports.

### April
The **Hong Kong International Film Festival** is a two-week film indulgence screening more than 240 films from around the world.

### June
The **International Dragon Boat Festival** honours the death of a man of scrupulous beliefs who threw himself into a river to protest against corrupt government.

### July
A number of small festivals from the **Hong Kong Comics Festival** to the **Book Fair** and the **Lan Kwai Beer & Food Festival**.

### August
The **Hungry Ghosts Festival** is when the gates of hell release 'hungry ghosts' to walk on Earth for two weeks. On the last day, offerings are burned for the ghosts and food is set out to send them back.

### September
Held on the 15th night of the eighth moon, the **Mid-Autumn Lantern Festival** remembers an uprising against the Mongols in the 14th century.

### November/December
From the end of November through December, downtown Hong Kong is transformed into a winter wonderland complete with 'Santa Town' during **Hong Kong Winterfest**.

## The Best of the Best

Of all the special events held annually, the Best of the Best Culinary Awards go straight to the heart of what Hong Kong is all about. The Chinese, and especially Hong Kongers, *love* to eat and they are among the most demanding of diners. Seafood in restaurants is plucked from a tank when it's as fresh as possible, vegetables are of the finest quality and presentation is everything. Little wonder this

⬥ *Food like you've never seen it before*

city is called the culinary capital of Asia; it's undoubtedly where you come for the best Chinese food in the world.

The Best of the Best Culinary Awards was launched in 2001 by the Hong Kong Tourism Board to showcase the diversity of Hong Kong's culinary arts and to highlight the vast selection of dishes available in this world-class cuisine. By stimulating creativity and competition, the Awards elevate culinary standards throughout the country and offer visitors a gastronomic experience that will last a lifetime.

These visitors flock into the city from around the world to see, taste and experience the best the chefs can offer and also the art of preparing Chinese meals for themselves. In 2005 a new series of gastronomic programmes to highlight the prize-winning restaurants and chefs was set up to immediately follow the Awards. This creates a citywide food festival showcasing 'the best of the best' with many of the award-winning restaurants offering special discounts. Visitors can also take part in culinary workshops to try their hand at creating old favourites or some of the new fusion creations.

The competition is broken down into four categories: deep-fried dishes; spicy dishes; vegetarian; and Chinese world fusion. Contestants use either traditional cooking methods or combine a variety of methods to produce innovative dishes. Of all the categories, the Chinese world fusion typifies Hong Kong best, a city with as colourful a blend of cultures as it has food choices.

ⓘ Be prepared when it comes to food in Hong Kong, for anything goes. Keep an open mind and enjoy the variety and diversity on offer, from upmarket restaurants to street stalls.

# History

Even though Hong Kong's story goes back thousands of years, historians usually begin with the last century and a half when Britain and China, then already trading partners, hit an impasse over the cost of silk and tea. During the 1800s, tea had become the British national drink and the only place it was grown was China. Similarly, silk was highly prized and China was the sole producer. Britain tried to encourage the Chinese to buy British goods, but they would have none of it—all they wanted was silver bullion in payment for silk and tea. The Chinese also forbade anyone to enter into their kingdom with the exception of a small trading depot at Canton.

As frustration built, the British traders found one thing the Chinese would buy, albeit secretly – Indian-grown opium. Before long, silver was flowing in the opposite direction as Chinese of all classes became enslaved to the drug. In retaliation, the Chinese emperor declared a ban on opium importing, but the British continued to smuggle it in. In 1939, the Chinese hit back by burning all supplies of opium stockpiled in Canton, thereby launching the first Opium War. However, Chinese war junks were no match for the Royal Navy and in humiliation the Chinese had to sign the Treaty of Nanking, which allowed the continued importation of opium and ceded Hong Kong Island in perpetuity to Britain. In the second Opium War (1856–8) Kowloon was added, and then the New Territories in 1898 on a 99-year lease.

Over the next century, Hong Kong's unique blend of Chinese life and British traditions developed and the economy flourished under an appointed governing body. As the 99-year lease began to run out, China launched a series of talks to define a new way of governing

Hong Kong, which was to return to China as a Special Administrative Region (SAR) guaranteeing its capitalist lifestyle and social system for at least 50 years after 1997.

Since the handover, there have been bumps, mistakes, unavoidable calamities as well as global misfortunes, but for the most part Hong Kong continues with life as usual. The city was hit hard by economic recession in the 1990s and had a number of policy setbacks as Communist 'control' tried to co-exist with Hong Kong economic freedom. One of the biggest setbacks was not politics but the eruption of SARS in the spring of 2003, the mysterious flu-like ailment that devastated China and Hong Kong. SARS dealt a major blow to the Hong Kong economy hitting retail trade, business and tourism hard. Tourism had already plummeted after September 11 as visitors fearful of long-distance travel stayed closer to home. Today, the city seems poised for a tourism renaissance.

Since its dramatic birth, Hong Kong has always been a city that thrived on hard work and tenacity, and that special HK energy shows no sign at all of fading.

◆ *Hong Kong's coastal location has been critical to its history*

## Lifestyle

If there's any one golden ideal in Hong Kong it's the Horatio Alger story, for this is a city that fairly abounds in rags-to-riches tales of entrepreneurs who created empires from scratch. People work very hard in Hong Kong – all part of an obsession they have with success. Immigrants share one dream: to make money quickly. So everything seems to move at lightning speed.

🔺 *Early morning tai chi in one of the parks*

When they do take a break, Hong Kongers seem to play with the same feverish intensity – whether it's betting on the horses or playing cricket. Dining together is one of their favourite pursuits and if you're invited to dinner it's highly unlikely it will be to your host's home. Most flats here are very small so social entertaining is usually at restaurants. These gatherings tend to be at large round tables in vast noisy establishments, where the food comes in relays and everyone shares. Ordering your own dish (as is common in the West) would be unthinkable.

Lunches downtown are usually in a hurry and are a bit of a shark-feeding frenzy. But this is just Hong Kong dining, and after a while most visitors are seduced.

## TRADITIONAL BELIEFS

While Western traditions are everywhere, superstitions still weave through daily life

Take a stroll through the Temple Street Night Market and you'll see Hong Kongers seated at small tables listening intensely as fortune tellers read their palms or consult their cards. Chinese take all this very seriously and will tell you that palm reading, fortune sticks, facial reading and other methods of future prediction go way back in time. The Chinese zodiac is consulted when young couples plan a family, since being born or married in a particular year can determine the whole course of a child's life. Perhaps the most persuasive belief is in feng shui ('wind and water'), based on the belief that wind and water were created by the gods and therefore reflect the will of the gods. It influences where parks are placed, tunnels dug, highways carved out, buildings located and even where graves are sited.

## Culture

Although Westerners may initially feel at home in Hong Kong, after a while they will realise that it is rooted in a very ancient Chinese tradition. The population is 95 per cent Chinese, with the vast majority being Cantonese.

Even though Hong Kong is a modern, capitalist society, it still holds strongly to the paternalistic, family oriented system established by China's most venerable sage, Confucius. He believed that all individuals are directly responsible for their fate, so a person should always think carefully before acting. With this kind of grounding, little wonder the Chinese have the work ethic they do along with traditional values that include respect for elders, reverence for ancestors and a belief in perseverance.

Within the family, parents will work extremely long hours to ensure their children get the best in health care and education so that one day they will look after their parents in their old age. Children grow up expecting to support their parents and to honour their ancestors by regularly visiting their graves and making offerings. Unlike the West, overt affection is not usually displayed; love and caring are expressed through acts of kindness, not words.

The lives of young people in Hong Kong are quite different from their Western counterparts. Since the cost of accommodation is high, they tend to live at home until they marry, and often even after marriage the couple continue living with parents. When they're courting, it is highly unlikely couples will be without

● *The very traditional style of Chinese opera*

siblings or relatives watching. The only romantic retreats are public parks. For those who need undisturbed passion, 'love motels' can be rented by the hour in Kowloon.

While it may appear that money is the major god worshipped in Hong Kong, religion does continue to play a big role in people's lives. Most are either Buddhist or Taoist with about 500,000 Christians and a handful of Muslims, Hindus, Sikhs and Jews. Throughout Hong Kong you will see people lighting incense at temple shrines or visiting ornate monasteries where nuns and monks are supported. Hong Kong, unlike China with its crackdown on Falun Gong, enjoys total freedom of religious practice.

While Western medicine is routinely practised, Chinese herbal medicine still remains popular and is surprisingly effective for universal complaints such as the common cold, 'flu, chronic backache, asthma and migraine headaches. Chinese medicine dates back 5,000 years and a visit to a Chinese herbalist is an enlightening experience. The herbalist will pull out of a battery of tiny drawers in a huge wall cupboard a wild assortment of powders, twigs and dried objects, and instruct you on how to prepare the cure. (You really don't want to know what you've been given, but the mixture often works like a charm.)

Chinese acupuncture is a common treatment in the West – especially for soft tissue injuries. In Hong Kong, it's used to treat long-term complaints by – according to the acupuncturist – using energy channels or meridians from the point of insertion to the area of complaint.

*View of the city from Victoria Peak*

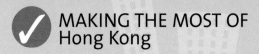
# MAKING THE MOST OF
Hong Kong

# Shopping

Hong Kong is a mecca for shopoholics, but even shopophobics are likely to buy something. Some of the best items are clothing, high tech goodies, electronics, jewellery, pearls, watches, spectacles and silk sheets. Credit cards are widely accepted except in the markets.

The main shopping areas are Central and Causeway Bay on Hong Kong Island and Tsim Sha Tsui (Nathan Road) in Kowloon. Many of the low-end clothing outlets and department stores are in Causeway Bay as well as warehouse sales, factory extras outlets and cheap jeans in Lee Garden Road. Best places for designer fashions are the shopping centres and malls. For browsers, budget shoppers and those who are as interested in plain old people-watching, the best places to start are Hong Kong's many open-air or covered markets. The biggest in the territory is the Temple Street Night Market in Yau Ma Tei for cheap clothes, knock-off watches, pirated CDs and DVDs, footwear and cookware. It's a good place to sample street food and perhaps visit one of the many fortune tellers who lay bare your future with the assistance of a trained bird. Stanley Market (in Stanley, on the southern part of Hong Kong Island) is as much a tourist destination as a place to shop, but it also has lots of good clothing bargains – including cashmere sweaters and rock-bottom priced pashminas.

Even though the city isn't the total bargain basement it once was, there are no sales taxes and shops offer great buys – particularly for anyone who likes to bargain. And you can haggle over price anywhere, except in department stores where prices are fixed. Those coming mainly to shop, should visit during end-of-season sales (January/February and July/August) when prices are slashed from 50 per cent to 90 per cent.

## THE BESPOKE BUBBLE

One of the many Hong Kong stories that refuses to die is that of bargain-priced suits tailored to perfection in just 24 hours. Perhaps the myth survives because if you shop around you can still find suits made in a day – but you wouldn't want to wear the end result in public.

The legend began in the 1950s when escapees from Shanghai, many of them tailors accustomed to stitching up quality garments, flooded into Hong Kong. Later, during the Korean and Vietnam wars, US soldiers coming through Hong Kong on R&R flocked to tailor shops looking for cheap, custom-made suits. Before long, English-speaking South Asians with tailoring experience were appearing all over Tsim Sha Tsui, catering to military personnel, tourists and local business people. Competition and cheap labour from the mainland bred Hong Kong's high-quality, low-price reputation and gave birth to the cheap 24-hour suit.

Today, a well-tailored garment in HK will cost as much as back home, but with a difference – the quality of the fit. A good suit today will take a minimum of three days and two fittings.

● Don't buy anything in a hurry and always shop around to compare prices. Be sure electronic items and cameras come with at least a one-year worldwide warranty and that all the accessories said to be included are in the box. If you want to buy authentic goods, shop in places where the HKTB logo is clearly displayed.

# Eating & drinking

A Chinese gourmet friend once said: 'We Chinese eat everything with legs and wings except tables and aeroplanes.' How true: the Chinese utilise everything that is vaguely edible and creatively spin it into a huge variety of regional styles that range from the subtle flavours of Guangzhou (Canton) to the chilli-laden stir fries of Sichuan. While there are no typical Hong Kong dishes, you can find a restaurant somewhere featuring the many shades of Chinese gastronomy (along with international cuisine, too).

Guangzhou-style dishes are subtle with delicate well-balanced flavours, neither salty nor greasy, and prepared by quick stir frying

⬥ *For a novel location try Jumbo, the famous floating restaurant*

**RESTAURANT CATEGORIES**

The following price ratings used throughout this book indicate the average price of a three-course meal for one without drinks

£ up to 100 HK$; ££ between 100–200 HK$; £££ above 200 HK$

and steaming. Typical dishes are *xiu ab* (roast duck, seasoned with spices and based in honey, soy and vinegar), *dung gua ton* (winter melon soup) and the universally loved *yum cha* (dim sum).

Shantou (Chui Chow) cuisine reflects a love of seafood with dishes such as *hai ji yu chi ton* (shark's fin soup) and exotic birds' nest soup. Typical dishes include *chui jau yu ton* (aromatic fish soup) and *chui jau lou sui ngoh* (soyed goose).

East Coast or Shanghai cuisine tends to be strongly flavoured and is usually stewed, fried or braised with a salty taste balanced by sweet flavours. Typical dishes include hot-and-sour soup, drunken chicken and braised eel. One of the cuisine's most famous dishes is hairy crab, a delicacy usually found only in autumn.

Rich, succulent Beijing cuisine is probably historically influenced by the Imperial Court and its most famous dish is *bak ging tin ab* (Peking duck). This cuisine uses strongly flavoured vegetables with lots of noodles, dumplings and bread instead of rice.

Sesame and chilli oil are common flavourings in Sichuan cuisine, which is the most spicy. Star anise, fennel, chilli, coriander and garlic add a zip to dishes that blend the five key flavours: sweet, sour, salty, peppery and chilli hot. Some of the culinary treasures are: *ma po deo fu* (grandmother's tofu) and *jeung cha ab* (duck smoked in camphor tea).

Hong Kongers love to eat and they have as many places (around 9,000 restaurants in the city) in which to indulge this favourite pastime as dishes to choose from. Traditionally some of the best and oldest restaurants are in major hotels, and these tend to be social and cultural centres – especially at weekends. The city has now embraced 'concept restaurants'. Some of these – such as Finds, which serves light Scandinavian food surrounded by faux igloo walls and chandeliers made of icicles – are a far cry from what you might expect. If you are looking for a cultural experience along with dinner, the *dai pai dong* (licensed mobile food stalls) are great, a kind of alfresco *chinois* dining. These stalls mainly appear after dark in places like the Temple Street Night Market. Most sell seafood such as fresh oyster omelette with spring onion and coriander. Some of the *dai pai dong* have moved indoors to places like Heng Tat on Lockhard Road in Wan Chi. The *laat jiu hai* (chilli crab) here will make you weep for joy.

You can spend a small fortune on dinner at Gaddi's in the Peninsula Hotel, but you can also eat for peanuts in Hong Kong if you go where the ordinary folk dine. Places like Cammy Restaurant in Mong Kok are filled with locals seated at wooden tables discussing and cussing and slurping up wonderful noodle soup, fried rice or veggie dishes. Noodle and congee shops are also everywhere (usually at ground level) and serve belly warming *juk* (congee rice porridge), the equivalent of Chinese fast-cum-comfort food, or filling helpings of chicken soup thick with noodles. Yum Cha houses have been around for 1,000 years and serve around 2,000 varieties of dim sum morning and noon. Dim sum dining is as much an event as a meal. Once you manage to grab a chair, you then watch for ladies with trolleys laden with steamer baskets filled with hot steamed buns, tarts, puddings, spring rolls and dumplings. Your choice is placed on a little dish and these are added up at the end of the meal. One of the best places to experience real, live Hong Kong dim sum is City Hall Maxim's Palace.

## THE RULES: DOS & DON'TS.

### DO ...

- place your chopsticks horizontally on the plate or table, not on your bowl
- spit out your bones or shells onto the table when eating fish or shellfish
- shovel your rice from your bowl instead of picking up rice grains with chopsticks
- say 'thank you' if someone puts food into your bowl
- stand up and lean over the table to get a bit of food on the other side.

### DON'T ...

- hold your chopsticks pointing straight up or point at anyone (it's very unlucky)
- fill your own tea cup before filling those of fellow diners
- take food from the main plate and put it directly in your mouth (put it in your bowl first)
- flip a whole fish over to get at the other side (it's unlucky; it symbolises the capsizing of a boat)
- start cleaning the table while others are still eating
- pick your teeth without covering your mouth.

# Entertainment & nightlife

Hong Kongers tend to carry their 'work hard' ethic into playtime, so there's no end of things to do after dark – from wine bars and dance clubs to Cantonese opera and avant-garde theatre. *HK Magazine* (which is free and appears each Friday) carries the latest cultural events in town. Many headliners include Hong Kong on their circuit, highbrow and lowbrow. Other night time activities include tours by

● *The painted face of a Cantonese opera star*

boat or bus, horse racing at Happy Valley, or romantic strolls at the top of The Peak or along the promenade of the Tsim Sha Tsui waterfront. For night time colour, the Temple Street Night Market and the Ladies' Market near the Mong Kok MTR Station are often open until after 22.00.

## BARS & CLUBS

The once wicked world of Suzie Wong may have faded into history, but there's still enough snap, crackle and pop to make things lively. True, it may not exactly be Bangkok, but you can still party 'til dawn at bars and discos, many of which don't really take off until after midnight. There are sophisticated piano bars, smoky jazz dens, elegant lounges, superstrobe discos and rowdy pubs.

In Central, the happening area is Lan Kwai Fong (also known as The Fong, or LKF) – a narrow alleyway that runs south from D'Aguilar Street and then doglegs west. Once home to rats and tenement housing, LKF has had a facelift and is now the hottest and trendiest place in town attracting celebs and the young and hip who have cash to spare with its funky music and good food. Trendsetters also like the SoHo (South Hollywood) district (along the Central/Mid-Levels Escalator), which continues to spawn upmarket ethnic eateries and bars. On weekend nights, Wan Chai is thick with partygoers and many of the clubs (such as the tacky-but-fun Strawberries) stay open past dawn every day of the week.

The pubs and bars of Causeway Bay are relatively tame compared with Wan Chai and LKF and there are a handful of bars in Quarry Bay around Tong Chong Street. Kowloon's night scene is more run-down than Central, but places along Knutsford Terrace make a claim to be Kowloon's Lan Kwai Fong. For full details check www.hkclubbing.com

❶ Expect overcrowding at the hippest places. Most clubs and discos will levy a cover charge, but this usually includes a complimentary drink.

## MUSIC, THEATRE & THE ARTS

It's best to pick up a copy of the youth-oriented *HK Magazine*, which lists everything that's going on. It's available at shops, restaurants, hotels and bars. Alternatively, check www.asia-city.com

*What's On–Hong Kong* is a leaflet published weekly by the HKTB listing what's happening in theatre, music and the arts. For special events and nightlife info, check *Where Hong Kong*, *CityLife* and *bc* – three free magazines published monthly.

## CINEMAS

Hong Kong has around 55 cinemas (with 185 screens) showing local films with English subtitles or Hollywood blockbusters dubbed into Cantonese. Almost all films shown in the city have both English and Chinese subtitles, but you can check to see if the film is in English in the cinema's Censorship licence. The *South China Morning Post* and *HK Magazine* list what's currently being shown.

❶ To book tickets for cultural events contact **Urbtix** ❶ 2111 5999 or check ⓦ www.urbtix.gov.hk
You can either pay by credit card in advance or reserve with a passport number. Urbtix also has windows at the HK City Hall, the HK Cultural Centre or many Tom Lee Music Stores.
Another booking venue for films, concerts and cultural events is **Cityline** ❶ 2317 6666 ⓦ www.cityline.com.hk

❿ *The streets are busy both day and night*

# Sport & relaxation

Hong Kong is the place to make tai chi, the ancient Chinese regimen designed to balance body and soul, part of your daily life. Both young and older practitioners meet every morning in downtown parks and open spaces to go through the languid motions – and visitors are encouraged to join in.

> ❶ Every Monday, Wednesday and Thursday at 08.00 you can take a complimentary 1-hour tai chi lesson (given in English) courtesy of the HK Tourism Board's Meet the People cultural programme. Just show up at the waterfront promenade outside the Hong Kong Cultural Centre on Tsim Sha Tsui near the Star Ferry.

For casual hikers, there are trails of varying difficulty in the city's many country parks. Serious hikers should check out the famous MacLehose Trail in the New Territories. The strenuous Lantau Trail on Lantau Island includes a 2½-hour climb to the top of Lantau Peak. The HKTB has trail maps and a hiking/wildlife guidebook plus recommended hikes on www.discoverhongkong.com

The best jogging trails are Victoria Park's track in Causeway Bay, Bowen Road, Harlech Road and the inside track at Happy Valley – that is if the horses aren't using it. Kowloon Park and the waterfront promenade along Tsim Sha Tsui and Tsim Sha Tsui East are also good.

## SPECTATOR SPORTS

If there's anything Hong Kongers love with a passion, it's horse racing and Happy Valley (the oldest racecourse in Asia outside of

China) is the place to be from September to mid-June. There's also a modern track in Sha Tin in the New Territories accommodating 90,000 spectators. Races usually take place Wednesday evenings and some Saturday and Sunday afternoons. Since racing is the only legal form of gambling in Hong Kong, the betting is both hot and heavy.

The Seven-A-Side Rugby Tournament (called The Sevens) held in March or April is probably the most popular annual sporting event. There are also several marathons such as the Hongkong-Shenzen Marathon (February) and the China Coast Marathon (March). The highlight for golfers is the Hong Kong Open Golf Championship and, for tennis, the Marlboro Championship.

🔺 *The betting is frenzied at Happy Valley*

## Accommodation

The cost of a roof over your head is higher in Hong Kong than in many Asian cities, but not as costly as Europe. To get the price range you want you should always book well in advance – especially if you plan to travel between March and April, and October and November. Major trade fairs at Hong Kong's expanded convention centre also gobble up hotel rooms at various times of the year.

You can book in advance using an Internet hotel agency such as Expedia.com, Travelocity, Hotels.com, Asiatravel.com, Asiahotels.com and Quikbook.com. It's important to shop around and compare rates at the Hong Kong Hotels Association website (www. hkha.com.hk) or individual hotel websites.

If you arrive without a reservation, contact the **Hong Kong Hotels Association** (🕿 2375 8380 or 🌐 wwww.hkha.org), or check the reservation centre inside Halls A and B on level 5 of the International Airport. They can book you into mid-range to top hotels at great savings.

🛈 When you make an online booking, be sure to get a confirmation number and a printout of any transaction.

### HOTELS & GUEST HOUSES

**Best Western Rosedale on the Park** **££** Right across from Victoria Park, this cyber hotel has a boutique atmosphere with mod-cons galore. ❸ 8 Shelter Street, Causeway Bay 🕿 2127 8606 🌐 www.rosedale.com.hk

**Bishop Lei International House** **££** In a residential area popular with expats and surrounded by good restaurants and bars, the small

**PRICE RATINGS**
Hotels in this book are graded according to the average price
for a double room per night.
£ up to HK$1,010; ££ HK$1,010–2,035; £££ above HK$2,035

rooms are offset by some fine harbour views. ⓐ 4 Robinson Road,
Mid-Levels ⓣ 2868 0828 ⓦ www.bishopleihtl.com.hk

**BP International ££** The BP stands for Baden-Powell – yes, he of the
Scouts (who own BP International). What's offered are comfortable,
clean rooms that are a little short on designer flair. A good place
if you're travelling with kids, not least because Kowloon Park is
extremely close. ⓐ 8 Austin Road, Tsim Sha Tsui ⓣ 2376 1111
ⓦ www.bpih.com.hk

**Eaton Hotel ££** Recently renovated, this has a great 4th-floor lobby
lounge, a rooftop pool and comfortable guest rooms with all
amenities. Near Temple Street Market. ⓐ 380 Nathan Road, Yau Ma
Tei ⓣ 2782 1818 ⓦ www.eaton-hotel.com

**Empire Hotel Kowloon ££** In a glass tower, this hotel (opened
in 2002) has a stylish contemporary décor and is convenient for
shopping in TST. State-of-the-art techy stuff plus indoor atrium
with pool and spa. ⓐ 62 Kimberley Road, Tsim Sha Tsui ⓣ 2685 3000
ⓦ www.asiastandard.com

**Metropark Hotel ££** Cheery, comfortable, contemporary with free
broadband Internet, a rooftop pool and great harbour views.

⊘ 148 Tung Lo Wan Road, Causeway Bay ⊙ 2600 1000
ⓦ www.metroparkhotel.com

**Regal Airport ££** This large hotel is a 5-minute walk to the airport
and has heaps of facilities – from a superb children's rec room to a
rotating art gallery. Rooms also available for day use.
⊘ 9 Cheong Tat Road, HK International Airport ⊙ 2286 8888
ⓦ www.regalhotel.com

**Jia Boutique Hotel ££–£££** HK's hippest boutique hotel, its stylish
rooms have every comfort and modern toy, plus there's free gym
access. ⊘ 1–5 Irving Street, Causeway Bay ⊙ 3196 9000
ⓦ www.jiahongkong.com

◆ *Take to the water for the best view of Hong Kong*

**Grand Hyatt Hong Kong £££** Sumptuous and up-to-the-minute, this is Hyatt's flagship hotel in Asia. Every service imaginable, including the largest outdoor pool in the city. ⓐ 1 Harbour Road, Wan Chai ⓣ 2588 1234 ⓦ www.hongkong.hyatt.com

**Kowloon Shangri-La £££** On the waterfront of Tsim Sha Tsui East, this recently renovated hotel has spacious rooms, great views and all the amenities and services you'd expect from a Shangri-La hotel. ⓐ 64 Mody Road, Tsim Sha Tsui ⓣ 2721 2111 ⓦ www.shangri-la.com

**The Peninsula £££** This is the oldest, grandest, most famous hotel in HK and a stay here is a never-to-be-forgotten event. Prices are very high but you get a Rolls-Royce to take you shopping, spacious rooms, incomparable service, a practice music room and the grand

Gaddi's Restaurant. **a** Salisbury Road, Tsim Sha Tsui
**t** 2920 2888 **w** www.peninsula.com

## HOSTELS & CAMPSITES

**Ascension House £** If you don't mind commuting by rail into the city, this hostel on a mountain in the jungle in the New Territories is one of the best deals you'll find. Clean dorm beds, three meals a day and laundry for good rates. **a** 33 Tao Fong Shan Road, Sha Tin **t** 2691 4196 **w** www.achouse.com

**Booth Lodge £** Run by the Salvation Army, Booth is clean, spartan and convenient to the Mass Transit Railway (MTR) and various markets. **a** 11 Wing Sing Lane, Yau Ma Tei **t** 2771 9266 **w** http://boothlodge.salvation.org.hk

**Hong Kong Hostel £** Quiet and clean, it's one of the best deals on HK Island. Most rooms have phones, fridges and TV. There are cooking and laundry facilities plus a computer room. **a** Flat A2, 3rd Floor, Paterson Building, 47 Paterson Street, Causeway Bay **t** 2895 1015 **w** www.wangfathostel.com.hk

**Jockey Club Mt Davis Youth Hostel £** HK's only 'official' hostel, this 163-bed facility on top of Mt Davis is clean and quiet with great views of Victoria Harbour. Call first. Cooking and laundry facilities. **a** Mt Davis Path, Kennedy Town **t** 2817 5715 **w** www.yha.org.hk

**Noble Hostel £** An immaculately clean, conveniently located guesthouse. All 45 rooms have a phone, fridge and AC. **a** Flat A3, 7th Floor, Great George Bldg, 27 Paterson Street, Causeway Bay **t** 2576 6148 **w** www.noblehostel.com.hk

**The Salisbury YMCA £** Not only is this excellent value but also it's terrific when travelling with kids. It's a 2-minute walk to the Star Ferry and TST subway, has suites for families, inexpensive café, kids swimming pool, indoor climbing wall and much more. ⓐ Salisbury Road, Tsim Sha Tsui ⓣ 2268 7000 ⓦ www.ymcahk.org.hk

**Camping £** There are several holiday camps in the New Territories managed by the Country & Marine Parks Authority. ⓣ 2420 0529 ⓦ http://parks.afcd.gov.hk; www.hadla.gov.hk

△ *Spend a lofty night at Ascension House*

# THE BEST OF HONG KONG

## TOP 10 ATTRACTIONS

- **Peak experience** Take the funicular tramway to the top of Victoria Peak for a view that will knock your socks off. Try it again at night (see page 64).

- **Tailored to a T** Scoot to the tailor and get measured for the best-fitting outfit in your wardrobe (see page 23).

- **Walled city** The Sam Tung Uk Museum – a restored Hakka walled village – takes you on a time trip to view life in the 18th century (see page 98).

- **The Tian Tan Buddha** is the world's largest seated outdoor bronze Buddha. Follow this with vegetarian lunch at the Po Lin Monastery (see pages 108–9).

- **Fortune smiles** There's no better place than superstitious HK to have your Chinese horoscope prepared at the Temple Street Night Market. (see page 81).

- **A different world** Take a breather from HK congestion to hike the remote regions of the New Territories to see abandoned villages and rice fields, sweeping vistas, beaches and old Taoist shrines (see pages 32 & 96).

- **A star is born** As HK's quintessential mode of travel, the Star Ferry is a must for a cheap harbour tour and great skyline pix (see page 76).

- **Morning meditation** After a quick introduction to tai chi, join the skilled practitioners in one of the city's parks (see page 65).

- **Party central** Rest up in the day, then dance until dawn in the discos and clubs of swinging Lan Kwai Fong (see page 29).

- **Cheap sightseeing** Ride the double-decker tram from one side of Hong Kong Island to the other.

🔻 *The Star Ferry*

Depending on the time you have, here are some short itineraries to tap into the best of Hong Kong.

### HALF-DAY: HONG KONG IN A HURRY

For a quick taster, stick to Central. Board the shuttle bus that will take you to the tram heading to Victoria Peak. Back down in Central, take the double-decker tram for a mini-tour of the island or try a walking tour. Finally, head for Pacific Place to splurge on designer duds or window shop.

### 1 DAY: TIME TO SEE A LITTLE MORE

Start with a dim sum breakfast at City Hall Maxim's Palace, then head for the Peak. Back at sea level, check out the tea ceremony at the Flagstaff House Museum of Tea Ware before taking the Star Ferry for a harbour experience to Kowloon. Lovers of gemstones should visit Yau Ma Tei's Jade Market. If you prefer clothes shopping, try Mong Kok's Ladies' Market. After a drink at the Peninsula's Felix, have dinner in Kowloon and end the day with the Symphony of Lights.

### 2–3 DAYS: SHORT CITY-BREAK

Visit the New Territories to see the Hong Kong Heritage Museum and the Sam Tung Uk Museum. Hike along the Ping Shan Heritage Trail to see some fascinating historical buildings and a glimpse of life hundreds of years ago. The Mai Po Wetlands with more than 300 bird species is an alternative. Explore some of the Outer Islands like Lamma to hike, swim or dine alfresco on the waterfront. It's also a good place for hikes. On Lantau island, climb up to the world's largest seated bronze Buddha, visit the Po Lin Monastery and for kids visit Hong Kong Disneyland.

## LONGER: ENJOYING HONG KONG TO THE FULL

Take a trip to Macau to see the mesh of Chinese and Portuguese cultures (and do a little gambling); plus visits to bordering cities like Shenzhen and Guangzhou in mainland China.

⬤ *The city shows off every night, with the Symphony of Lights*

# Something for nothing

Some of the best things in Hong Kong life are free – including panoramic views of the city you catch from the public viewing gallery on the 43rd floor of the Bank of China tower in Central. There are great views too on several hikes in the New Territories, including the MacLehose and Wilson Trails.

The Central/Mid-Levels escalator (the world's longest) is another freebie, although it may amuse kids more than adults.

On Lantau Island, there are walking trails galore and for the grand finale a 260-step climb to yet another superlative – the Tian Tan Buddha.

HK has a Meet the People programme, where you can learn tai chi, and about pearls, jade, Chinese antiques and more – for free.

Take a walk around the Ng Tung Chai Waterfall and streams just north of Tai Mo Shan, HK's tallest mountain. Southwest of the village of Ng Tung Chai, the Kadoorie Farm & Botanic Garden is a conservation and teaching centre with lovely gardens.

The Hong Kong Zoological and Botanical Gardens is a collection of sculptures, fountains, greenhouses, a zoo and a wonderful aviary. The Bird Garden on Yuen Po Street is set inside a Chinese courtyard filled with a multitude of birds and cages for sale. Like many other places, HK has a day (Wednesdays) when admission is free at most museums.

> ❶ The HKTB has free booklets (with maps) called *Hong Kong Walks* and *Hong Kong Unique Tours and Hiking Tours.*
> The Hong Kong Tourism Board's Visitor Information & Services Centres have full information on Meet the People programmes.

The waterfront Tsim Sha Tsui East Promenade is a great place to jog or stroll during the day and an eye-popping vista onto illuminated Central at night. For film buffs, the promenade has a new Avenue of the Stars that pays homage to the local film industry and its stars. You can also watch the Symphony of Lights here – a spectacular sound-and-light show utilising several buildings in Hong Kong's skyline. Dramatic lights dance and flash nightly for 20 minutes from 20.00.

● *Bird cages jostle on Bird Street*

## When it rains

In this humid subtropical climate, don't be surprised if you hit a
shower or two. In spring, the rain can be torrential providing a good

● *There are tea appreciation classes for serious tea drinkers*

excuse for indoor activities – starting with a dim sum breakfast in one of the city's livelier spots (City Hall Maxim's Palace in Central, for example). From here, you can hit the huge variety of museums: a wine museum, racing museum, museum of history, even a pawnshop museum in Macau. The Hong Kong Heritage Museum is a must where, in addition to all the treasures, you can visit the Cantonese Opera Heritage Hall, watch old operas on video with English subtitles and virtually make yourself up as a Cantonese opera character on computer. There's also a Police Museum (free) in Wan Chai Gap that tells the history of the HK police force, narcotics and Triads.

No one knows tea quite like the Chinese, but you can catch a glimmer in a Chinese Tea Appreciation class (free) – like the one run by Mr Ip Wing-chi at the Lock Cha Tea Shop – and learn about varieties, proper preparation and tea-drinking etiquette. Next door in the Flagstaff House Museum of Tea Ware is a mini-museum with a collection of rare teapots.

If Hong Kong is anything, it's shopping mall heaven. For upmarket shops, Central has the brand-new ifc mall located next to Hong Kong Station, Pacific Place and Shanghai Tang, while Times Square and Jardine's Crescent have lower-priced clothing. Not so well known are the micro malls crammed into old buildings or above MTR stations where you can find designer clothes, funky footwear and kooky accessories. Best times to shop are between 15.00 and 22.00 at places like the Up Date Mall in Tsim Sha Tsui, the Trendy Zone in Mong Kok and the Beverley Commercial Centre in Tsim Sha Tsui.

At the day's end, visit one of HK's British pubs for a happy hour that often stretches on ... It's a great way to meet locals and wait for the showers to end.

# On arrival

Hong Kong is 8 hours ahead of GMT and does not have daylight saving. At high noon in HK on a Monday in the winter when daylight saving time doesn't apply, time at home is as follows:

**Australia** (Sydney) 15.00 Monday; (Perth) noon, Monday
**New Zealand** 16.00 Monday
**South Africa** 18.00 Monday
**UK** 05.00 Monday
**USA** Eastern (New York) 23.00 Sunday; Central Time 20.00 Sunday; Mountain Time 17.00 Sunday; Pacific Time (San Francisco) 20.00 Sunday.

## ARRIVING

### By air

**Hong Kong International Airport** ( 2181 0000  www.hongkongairport.com) was considered the world's largest civil engineering project when it opened in mid-1988 and is the largest covered space in the world. It sits on Chek Lap Kok, a small island off the northern coast of Lantau, and is connected to the mainland by several spans including Tsing Ma Bridge, one of the world's largest suspension bridges. The airport is about 32 km (20 miles) from Hong Kong's central business district. It's two runways operate 24 hours a day and the baggage handling system delivers bags in approximately 10 minutes.

As the latest in design, the airport combines a pleasant ambience with a tranquil green environment plus facilities and services that are excellent – the usual cafeterias and restaurants, lounges, a beauty salon, shower rooms, foot massage, pharmacy and business centre. Banks and ATMs are available in the arrival and departure halls.

The dedicated Airport Express runs from 05.50 to 01.15 daily with trains coming at 12-minute intervals. It takes about 24 minutes to get into Central. There is also free in-town check-in and shuttle bus service available in Hong Kong and Kowloon for Airport Express passengers as well as free porter service at all the Airport Express stations. **Cityflyer Airbuses** (🕽 2873 0818 🅦 www.citybus.com.hk) has ticket counters in the airport arrivals hall with buses departing every 10 to 30 minutes. Fares cost between HK$33 and HK$45 depending on where you go; the exact fare is required.

◔ Hong Kong International Airport's 1.3 km-long passenger terminal

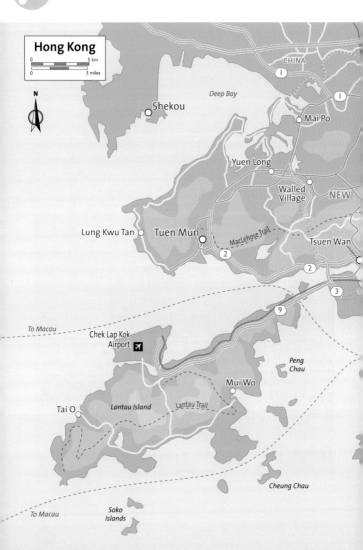

**Hong Kong**

0 — 5 km
0 — 3 miles

N

CHINA

Deep Bay

1

1

Shekou

Mai Po

Yuen Long

Walled
Village

NEW

Lung Kwu Tan

Tuen Mun

Maclehose Trail

Tsuen Wan

2

2

3

9

To Macau

Chek Lap Kok
Airport

Peng
Chau

Mui Wo

Tai O

Lantau Island

Lantau Trail

Cheung Chau

To Macau

Soko
Islands

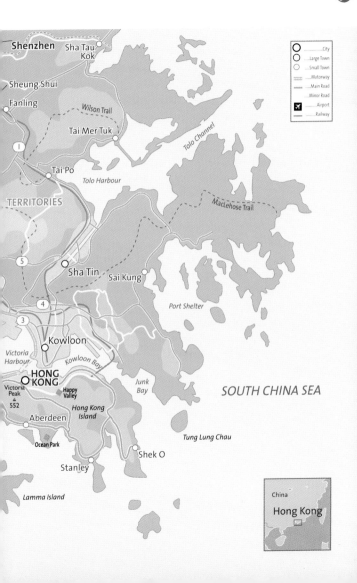

| | |
|---|---|
| ○ | City |
| ○ | Large Town |
| ○ | Small Town |
| | Motorway |
| | Main Road |
| | Minor Road |
| ✈ | Airport |
| | Railway |

Shenzhen

Sha Tau Kok

Sheung Shui

Fanling

Wilson Trail

Tai Mer Tuk

Tolo Channel

Tai Po

Tolo Harbour

TERRITORIES

MacLehose Trail

Sha Tin

Sai Kung

Port Shelter

Kowloon

Kowloon Bay

Victoria Harbour

HONG KONG

Victoria Peak 552

Junk Bay

SOUTH CHINA SEA

Happy Valley

Hong Kong Island

Aberdeen

Ocean Park

Tung Lung Chau

Stanley

Shek O

Lamma Island

China

Hong Kong

The **Airport Shuttle** (☏ 2735 7823) provides door-to-door service between the airport and major hotels. Tickets are available at a counter in the arrivals hall and cost HK$120. It takes about 30 to 40 minutes to reach Kowloon.

Taxis are always available and are relatively inexpensive in town but rather costly from the airport. They take about 30 to 45 minutes to Kowloon and cost around HK$300.

ⓘ For details on times for buses and trains fares visit
ⓦ www.hongkongairport.com and click on 'Passenger guide'.

Many people are aware that air travel emits $CO_2$ which contributes to climate change. You may be interested in the possibility of lessening the environmental impact of your flight through the charity Climate Care, which offsets your $CO_2$ by funding environmental projects around the world. Visit www.climatecare.org

## BY RAIL

Unless you're coming from the west via China, it's unlikely you'd arrive in Hong Kong by train. That said, the Beijing–Kowloon railway provides a direct link between these two cities and takes about 26 hours.

## BY SEA

It's also unlikely you will arrive by sea, unless it's with one of about 30 international cruise ships that dock at the Ocean Terminal in Tsim Sha Tsui. However, you can arrive from Macau by ferry (see pages 121–2).

## BY ROAD

Again, there are no highway links except from mainland China. City bus routes link the Shenzen economic zone and Hong Kong, and there's a coach service from Guangzhou.

## FINDING YOUR FEET

The biggest problem a visitor may have to deal with when visiting HK is the weather – particularly in the summer when it's stiflingly humid. Dress lightly but always carry something to throw over your shoulders when you go into a restaurant, since the air conditioning may be more suitable for penguins than people.

Despite its size and frenzied intensity, Hong Kong is a safe city and visitors feel secure walking almost anywhere, even at night – although it's best to use common sense and stick to well-lit areas. In most of the heavily touristy areas like Tsim Sha Tsui and Wan Chai, police patrol to watch out for pickpockets who work in gangs.

❶ It's wise to keep your valuables in the hotel safe along with your passport, and carry with you only what you need.

## ORIENTATION

People not familiar with Asia might think Hong Kong is just one island or one city, but it's actually divided into four distinct parts: Hong Kong Island, Kowloon Peninsula, the New Territories and the outlying islands. The whole area is known as the SAR (Special Administrative Region) and much of it is mountainous.

Both Hong Kong Island and Kowloon are further subdivided into districts with Central being the prime business and financial district. The others are Causeway Bay, Western and Wan Chai.

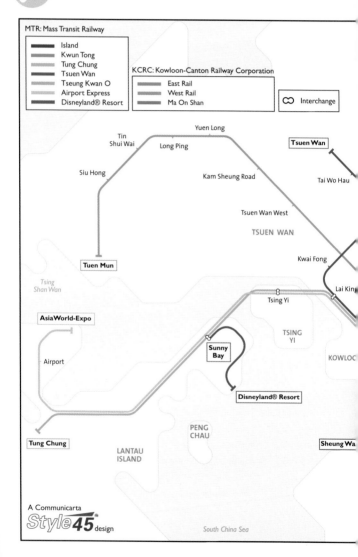

MTR: Mass Transit Railway

| | |
|---|---|
| | Island |
| | Kwun Tong |
| | Tung Chung |
| | Tsuen Wan |
| | Tseung Kwan O |
| | Airport Express |
| | Disneyland® Resort |

KCRC: Kowloon-Canton Railway Corporation

| | |
|---|---|
| | East Rail |
| | West Rail |
| | Ma On Shan |

∞ Interchange

Yuen Long

Tin Shui Wai

Long Ping

**Tsuen Wan**

Siu Hong

Kam Sheung Road

Tai Wo Hau

Tsuen Wan West

TSUEN WAN

**Tuen Mun**

Kwai Fong

Tsing Shan Wan

Lai Kin

**AsiaWorld-Expo**

Tsing Yi

Airport

TSING YI

KOWLOO

**Sunny Bay**

**Disneyland® Resort**

**Tung Chung**

PENG CHAU

**Sheung Wa**

LANTAU ISLAND

A Communicarta

Style45 design

South China Sea

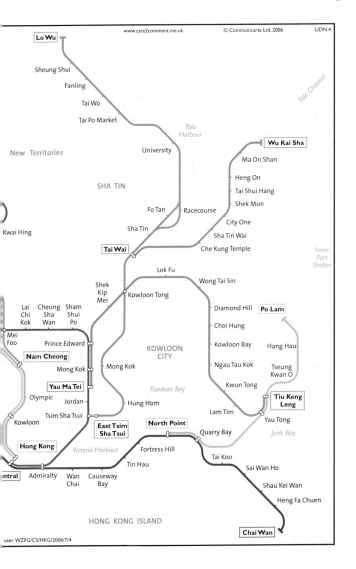

Lo Wu

Sheung Shui

Fanling

Tai Wo

Tai Po Market

New Territories

*Tolo Harbour*

University

*Tolo Channel*

Wu Kai Sha

Ma On Shan

Heng On

Tai Shui Hang

Shek Mun

City One

Sha Tin Wai

Che Kung Temple

*Inner Port Shelter*

SHA TIN

Fo Tan    Racecourse

Sha Tin

Tai Wai

Kwai Hing

Lok Fu

Wong Tai Sin

Diamond Hill    Po Lam

Choi Hung

Kowloon Bay    Hang Hau

Ngau Tau Kok    Tseung Kwan O

Kwun Tong

Shek Kip Mei

Kowloon Tong

KOWLOON CITY

*Kowloon Bay*

Lai Chi Kok    Cheung Sha Wan    Sham Shui Po

Mei Foo

Prince Edward

Nam Cheong

Mong Kok    Mong Kok

Yau Ma Tei

Olympic    Jordan

Kowloon    Tsim Sha Tsui

Hung Hom

Lam Tim

Tiu Keng Leng

Yau Tong

*Junk Bay*

Hong Kong

East Tsim Sha Tsui    North Point

*Victoria Harbour*    Quarry Bay

Fortress Hill    Tai Koo

Central    Admiralty    Wan Chai    Causeway Bay

Tin Hau

Sai Wan Ho

Shau Kei Wan

Heng Fa Chuen

HONG KONG ISLAND

Chai Wan

In Kowloon, tourists are usually most familiar with Tsim Sha Tsui (where most of the hotels, museums and shops are) along with Tsim Sha Tsui East, Mong Kok and Yau Ma Tei. Since these areas are so compact, Hong Kong is easy to navigate.

The largest area in the SAR is the New Territories, which start at the northern edge of Kowloon and stretch all the way to the Chinese border. Back in the 1960s, this was a highly rural area made up of vast green stretches dotted with small villages and farms and even though much still remains uninhabited, the Territories have changed enormously. Huge public-housing projects have pushed the population up to almost half the total number of people in Hong Kong.

While visitors usually only get to four or five of the outlying islands, there are actually 260 in all, most of them barren and uninhabited. Cheung Chau, Lantau and Lamma are the most popular and accessible.

**GETTING AROUND**

HK is definitely a city for walkers. Get a good street map (available free from HKTB or your hotel) and find the main thoroughfares, major roads and streets. On Hong Kong Island, Des Voeux Road, Queen's Road and Connaught Road are the principal streets with Hennessy Road and Gloucester Road leading east through Wan Chai to Causeway Bay. On Kowloon side, Nathan Road stretching north is the most important artery with Salisbury Road running east and west from the Star Ferry through Tsim Sha Tsui. There's also a promenade along the waterfront.

Public transport is safe, inexpensive and highly reliable and will let you get to almost anywhere you want to go within an hour. Just be sure to avoid rush hours (08.00 to 10.00 and 17.00 to 19.00).

ⓘ Buses require exact change, so check the fare before you board.

The cleanest, fastest and most efficient way to get around is via the **Mass Transit Railway** (MTR) (ⓣ 2881 8888 ⓦ www.mtr.com.hk). This system is always on time. The network is made up of five interconnected lines: blue, red, green, purple and yellow (see map, pages 54–5). Trains run every 2 to 10 minutes from around 06.00 to approximately 01.00. The MTR is fully automated. Just slip in your

● *The Star Ferry offers good value and unbeatable atmosphere*

Octopus Card (see below) and the turnstile will automatically deduct the fare from the balance on the card. For short trips, use the Star Ferry at a quarter the cost.

### OCTOPUS CARD

For more than a 1- or 2-day stay, use the Octopus Card for getting around. This is valid on most forms of transportation and will even allow you to make small purchases at some retail outlets such as 7-Eleven. You can buy Octopus cards at ticket offices or customer services centres in MTR, Kowloon–Canton Railway (KCR) or Light Rail Transit (LTR) stations.
Octopus Cards ☎ 2266 2266 ⓦ www.octopuscards.com

### CAR HIRE

Because HK public transportation is so good and traffic so frenzied, most people opt not to hire a car. For trips to the New Territories there are a number of companies that will rent on a daily, weekend or weekly rate (visit Hong Kong Yellow Pages at www.yp.com.hk). Most firms accept International Driving Permits or driving licences from your home country. Drivers must be at least 25 years of age. For a car with a driver, check **Ace Hire Car Service** ☎ 2572 7663 ⓦ www.acehirecar.com.hk

▶ *A tram will take you up Hong Kong's highest peak*

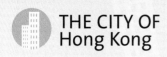

# THE CITY OF
# Hong Kong

# Hong Kong Island

Looking at images of Hong Kong, the first impression is that of a dense forest of skyscrapers and nothing more. But this is far from the reality. Hong Kong is actually a collection of neighbourhoods, each with a special character.

Central, in the very north of Hong Kong Island, is where the colony began in 1842. Today it is the seat of government and the most important financial district.

Within Central are smaller neighbourhoods such as Lan Kwai Fong (LKF), which is the hottest new entertainment area playing host to a range of restaurants and bars. These venues are magnets to people in their 20s and 30s.

SoHo (South Hollywood) is also a relatively new dining-and-nightlife district but a little quieter and more sane than LKF.

Hovering over Central, Victoria Peak is the island's most famous mountain and most exclusive address.

To the east of Central, Wan Chai and Causeway Bay are where you find the best in shopping and nightlife. To the west is Sheung Wan – an older, more distinctly Chinese neighbourhood where you will find antiques, funeral shops, Chinese medicine and those omnipresent 'chop' makers.

Aberdeen, on the south side of Hong Kong Island, was once a fishing village but is now a forest of high-rises and housing projects. It's also where you can still find sampans and Jumbo, the famous floating restaurant, as well as Ocean Park with its aquarium and amusement rides.

Stanley, on the quiet south side of the islands, was also a fishing village but is now the best discount marketplace for anything from shoes to souvenirs and silk suits.

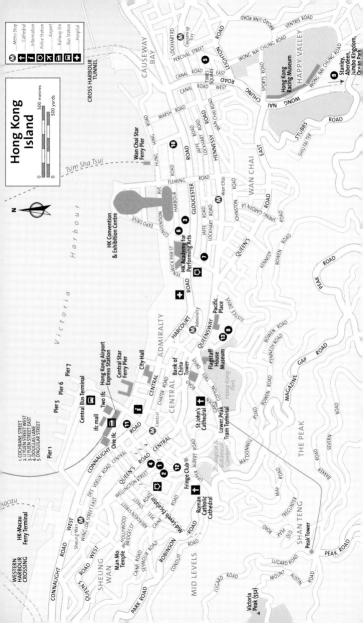

# Hong Kong Island

Metro Stop
Cathedral
Information
Police Station
Airport
Railway Stn
Bus Station
Hospital

0    500 metres
0    500 yards

N

1. COCHRANE STREET WEST
2. LI YUEN STREET WEST
3. LI YUEN STREET EAST
4. DOUGLAS STREET
5. D'AGUILAR STREET

CROSS HARBOUR TUNNEL

WESTERN HARBOUR CROSSING

HK-Macau Ferry Terminal

Macau

Victoria Harbour

Tsim Sha Tsui

CAUSEWAY BAY

HAPPY VALLEY

Hong Kong Racing Museum

WONG NAI CHUNG

Stanley, Aberdeen, Jumbo Kingdom, Ocean Park

WAN CHAI

Wan Chai Star Ferry Pier

HK Convention & Exhibition Centre

HK Academy for Performing Arts

ADMIRALTY

Hong Kong Airport Express Station

Central Star Ferry Pier

City Hall

Central Bus Terminal

Two ifc
ifc mall
One ifc

Pier 1
Pier 5
Pier 6
Pier 7

Bank of China Tower

Pacific Place

Flagstaff House Museum

Hong Kong Park

CENTRAL

SHEUNG WAN

Man Mo Temple

Mid-Levels Escalator

Fringe Club

Roman Catholic Cathedral

St John's Cathedral

Lower Peak Tram Terminal

Zoological & Botanical Gardens

MID LEVELS

THE PEAK

SHAN TENG

Peak Tower

Victoria Peak (552)

PEAK ROAD

LUGARD ROAD

## SIGHTS & ATTRACTIONS

### Bank of China Tower

This building is worth seeing not least because it's the best-known modern architectural symbol on the island and was designed by the well-known architect I M Pei. What makes a visit to it even more worthwhile is knowing a little about the controversy it has stirred up since its conception. Hong Kong is obsessed by feng shui and the 70-storey building's sharp angles were rumoured to be a symbolic mainland dagger aimed at the heart of Hong Kong that directed hostility towards Government House. The two antennae on top of the building were said to resemble incense burned for the dead. All this bad feng shui was also said to have affected the excellent feng shui of the HSBC Building – at least until Lee Ka-shing built the Cheung Kong Center between them and restored much of the harmony and energy flow.

ⓦ www.bochk.com

### Jumbo Kingdom

Located in Aberdeen, this area is famous for its recently re-invented 'kingdom' – home to a colourful floating seafood restaurant-cum-shopping venue, and a flotilla of junks interspersed with fishing boats and yachts. This is the place to hire a sampan (usually manned by a woman!) for a tour around the harbour to glimpse what life is like living on a junk.

ⓦ www.jumbo.com.hk

---

◗ *Bank of China Tower*

### Mid-Levels Escalator

One of the oddest attractions in Hong Kong, this is a series of 20 escalators and three 'travelators' (moving walkways) that alternate going up and down. Originally built to ease traffic congestion and help people living in the Mid-Levels region to get home without climbing hills, it is now the best way to get to the hip bars, antique stores and international restaurants of the SoHo area. From the top of the elevator, it's about a 20-minute walk to the Zoological and Botanical Gardens.

### Ocean Park

Close to Jumbo Kingdom is this combo amusement and marine park. It has a first-class aquarium and zoo where you can see pandas, walk the dinosaur trail and wander through a magical butterfly house. Well worth an afternoon visit.
☎ 2552 0291 🌐 www.oceanpark.com.hk

### Victoria Peak

This is Hong Kong Island's highest peak. So naturally that makes it the best place to take those classic shots of the city – especially if it is a clear day. A century ago, getting to the top of the peak meant a 3-hour trip in sedan chairs for the rich who lived there. Today, the Peak tram runs every 10 to 20 minutes for the 8-minute trip. At the top, there's **Madame Tussaud's** wax museum (🌐 ww.madame-tussauds.com.hk), **Ripley's Believe it or Not!** (🌐 www.thepeak.com.hk), plus the **Peak Explorer** (also 🌐 www.thepeak.com.hk) – a motion-simulator theatre that shakes and rolls to simulate racing cars or rollercoasters or whatever is on the screen. More tranquil is a circular hike through banyan trees and lush vegetation in **Victoria Park**.

### Zoological & Botanical Gardens

Come in the early morning and you can either observe (or take part in) the calming meditative tai chi exercises. Quiet pathways lined with semitropical trees and flowers lead to a zoo and an aviary with more than 300 species of birds.

ⓐ Upper Albert Road (opposite Government House); enter on Garden Road ⓣ 2530 0155 ⓦ www.lcsd.gov.hk

## CULTURE

### Flagstaff House Museum of Tea Ware

Whether tea intrigues you or not, the tea ceremony is an integral part of Chinese culture. This museum is the oldest colonial building in Hong Kong and is the best place to see 1846 architecture. You can marvel at some of the 600-piece collection of tea ware or buy replicas in the gift shop.

ⓐ 10 Cotton Tree Drive ⓣ 2869 0690 ⓦ www.lcsd.gov.hk

### Man Mo Temple

This is one of the oldest and most famous temples in Hong Kong and is named after two deities: one (Man Tai) the god of literature, and the other (Mo Tai) the god of war. The whole place has a mysterious atmosphere with giant incense cones suspended from the ceiling, worshippers lighting more cones and fortune tellers waiting to advise you of your fate.

ⓐ 124–126 Hollywood Road ⓣ 2540 0350

## RETAIL THERAPY

❶ If you are coming to Hong Kong to shop, then do beware of allowing yourself to fall prey to opportunists intent on obtaining your money under false pretences. Check that the shop or service provider displays a QTS (Quality Tourism Service) sticker, which identifies shops and restaurants that provide good service. The aim of the QTS Scheme, an initiative of the Hong Kong Tourism Board, is to give consumers protection. ⓦ www.info.gov.hk

**Hollywood Road** Most of Hong Kong's reputable antique shops are here. You can find luxury ticket items such as Ming dynasty vases, furniture and jewellery. ⓐ Hollywood Road

### LABELS TO LOOK FOR
When you're thinking of the big fashion centres on the planet, Hong Kong doesn't usually spring to mind. That said, there are some hot young designers that are really making waves.

- Lulu Cheung has nine stores in Hong Kong and China, and features classy womenswear.
- Barney Cheung is in the global spotlight with his pricey couture creations.
- Ruby Li creates designs with young street attitude.
- Johanna Ho is a big up-and-comer currently getting lots of recognition.
- Pacino Wan is probably the best known for his tongue-in-cheek creations; he's been called 'the most imaginative designer in Hong Kong'.

**ifc mall** This three-level shopping complex has high-end shops and restaurants. ❷ 8 Finance Street, Central ❶ 2295 3308 ⓦ www.ifc.com.hk

🔺 *The Mid-Levels Escalator is practical and fun!*

**The Lanes** This is shopping as old as Hong Kong itself. Here stalls sell just about everything from watches and toys to clothes and souvenirs. A good place to bargain hunt. ➋ Three narrow alleyways in Central – Douglas Lane, Li Yuen Street East and Li Yuen Street West – which run parallel to each other between Des Voeux and Queen's Roads

**Pacific Place** Go here if you are seeking a sleek, chic and well-designed place to shop. You'll find popular department stores like Lane Crawford, Sogo and Marks & Spencer, as well as smart clothing boutiques, restaurants and hotels. ➋ 88 Queensway, Central ➊ 2844 8988 ⓦ www.pacificplace.com.hk

## TAKING A BREAK

### Budget bites
**The Good Luck Thai Café £ ❶** A highly popular place tucked down a side street in LKF. It serves low-cost but tasty Thai food. ➋ 13 Wing Wah Lane, Lan Kwai Fong ➊ 2877 2971

**The Noodle Box £ ❷** This establishment has every kind of noodle you'd want plus a generous happy hour (15.30–18.00) when the noodle dishes sell for HK$30. Try the green papaya salad as a side. ➋ 30–32 Wyndham Lane, Central ➊ 2536 0571

### Anything to drink?
Tea may be traditional in this part of the world, but tell that to the crowd hanging out at all those Hong Kong Starbucks. Be it tea or

---

◀ *You can get traditional clothes made-to-measure*

coffee, those of you in need of refreshments at somewhere a little less international should try the places below.

**Cova £** This is a chain to look out for in Hong Kong; you get salads and sandwiches with your beverage.

**rbt £** Standing for 'real brewed tea' this chain, which has several outlets in Hong Kong, serves Taiwanese tea, a recent fad.

**Café Zambra ££** ❸ An educational break as well as a great cup of coffee – you learn all about roasting and grinding beans here. ⓐ 239 Jaffe Road, Wan Chai ⓣ 2535 9198

**Luk Yu Tea House ££** ❹ This art deco Cantonese restaurant is the most famous teahouse in Hong Kong complete with period spittoons. You can try the whole range of teas here from jasmine flavoured to daffodil, but the place is even more famous for its dim sum served 07.00–17.30. ⓐ 24–26 Stanley Street, Central ⓣ 2523 5464

## AFTER DARK

### Restaurants
**Bo Kung £** ❺ There's usually no problem finding a vegetarian entrée in most Cantonese restaurants. However, Bo Kung, which is dedicated to vegetarians, has meals so cleverly put together you're hardly aware they are vegetarian. ⓐ Times Square, 12th floor, 1 Matheson Street, Causeway Bay ⓣ 2506 3377

**Open Kitchen £** ❻ Touting an international menu with anything from laksa to lamb chops, this is one of the better bargains in town

– not least because you get a great view along with your buffet selection. ⓐ Hong Kong Arts Centre (6th floor), 2 Harbour Road, Wan Chai ⓣ 2827 2923

**Bebek Bengil 3 ££** ❼  Before hitting Wan Chai's nightlife options, dinner here is a soothing experience with low lighting, Balinese music and a room full of teak. Try the steamed fish in banana leaf, satay or those creamy southeast Asian curries. ⓐ The Broadway, 5th floor, 54–62 Lockhart Road, Wan Chai ⓣ 2217 8000

**Café TOO ££** ❽  Along with the setting overlooking Hong Kong Park, this is one of the better buffets in town with an international assortment of choices from French and continental to Thai, Japanese and Indian. ⓐ Island Shangri-La, Pacific Place, Supreme Court Road, Central ⓣ 2820 8571 ⓦ www.shangri-la.com

**Lucy's ££** ❾  After a hard day haggling in Stanley Market, Lucy's is a small, cosy spot just off Stanley Market where you can choose from a short menu that offers the freshest choices in season. The daily special is a good bet. ⓐ 64 Stanley Main Street, Stanley ⓣ 2813 9055

**The Viceroy ££** ❿  Lovely terrace dining area with romantic views of the harbour. An upmarket restaurant with good Indian food and a menu that changes regularly. Oh, and there's sitar music to add to the atmosphere. ⓐ Sun Hung Kai Centre (2nd floor), 30 Harbour Road, Wan Chai ⓣ 2827 7777

**Hunan Garden £££** ⓫  Like spicy food? Hunan cuisine tends to be even spicier than Sichuan and this place is a real find. Not only do

you get authentic dishes but also a great view of the harbour.
📍 The Forum, 3rd floor, Exchange Square, Central. 📞 2868 2880

**M at the Fringe £££** 🔟 A great place for dinner before an evening
of experimental drama in English at the Fringe Theatre below the
restaurant. Artsy décor and excellent eclectic international cuisine
with an ever-changing menu. 📍 2 Lower Albert Road, Central
📞 2877 4000 🌐 www.m-restaurantgroup.com

**Petrus £££** 🔟 If you're not knocked out by the
Mediterranean/French cuisine, you will be by the view from
the 56th-floor restaurant in the Island Shangri-La. Seasonal
ingredients are blended by a creative fusion and you'll find one
of the best wine lists in Hong Kong. This is an expensive night out
for a special occasion. 📍 Pacific Place, Supreme Court Road, Central
📞 2820 8590 🌐 www.shangri-la.com

### Bars & clubs

**Agave** It's said the best margaritas in town can be found here along
with more than 100 imported tequilas. This open-fronted, lively
Mexican bar has a happy hour that lasts 17.00–20.30. 📍 33 D'Aguilar
Street, LKF, Central 📞 2521 or 2010

**Dragon-1** For something a little different, you can mingle with caged
birds on a huge terrace over Wyndham Street. 📍 60 Wyndham
Street, Central 📞 3110 1222

*▶ Street cafés offer plenty of local flavour*

**Dublin Jack** About as close as you get to a genuine Irish pub. Smoke-free and very popular. ⓐ 37–43 Cochrane Street, Central ⓣ 2543 0081

**Groovy Mule** Dancer alert! There's an infectious atmosphere here, where everyone seems to be dancing – including the waiters who groove on the bar every so often. ⓐ 37–39 Lockhart Road, Wan Chai ⓣ 2527 2077

**1/5** A classy place with lots of glamour and those off-duty suits. ⓐ Starcrest, 9 Star Street, Wan Chai ⓣ 2217 8330

### Pop & jazz
**The Blue Door Jazz Club** is a serious jazz venue with excellent music. ⓐ 37–42 Cochrane Street, Central ⓣ 2858 6555

**Bohemian Lounge** Great place for a drink. What's more, if you go on Thursday after 21.00 or Friday and Saturday after 22.00 you'll catch some great live jazz. ⓐ 3–5 Old Bailey Street, SoHo ⓣ 2526 6099

### Performing arts
It may, at first sight, seem that Hong Kong is a bit of a cultural wasteland. But take note: appearances can be deceiving and this impression is not accurate. There are a number of well-funded performing arts companies with a range of options. For current concerts, check out *HK Magazine*.

**Hong Kong Academy of Performing Arts** You can see it all here: dance, music, drama, television and film. Both student and professional companies stage their work at this venue as well as local and visiting companies. Check out the free happy hour performances and lunchtime concerts. 🅐 1 Gloucester Road, Wan Chai 🅣 2584 8500 🅦 www.hkapa.edu

**Hong Kong Convention & Exhibition Centre** The venue for pop and rock concerts. Check its website for up-and-coming events. Alternatively, contact the Centre direct. 🅐 1 Harbour Road, Wan Chai 🅣 2582 8888 🅦 www.hkcec.com.hk

**The Fringe Club** Here you'll find avant-garde performances by home-grown talent. What's more, the theatre is the principal venue for the annual CityJan festival which features live music, art and photography exhibitions (January and February). It's best to check out the listings – everything from chanteuses to rock bands to jazz can be playing. 🅐 2 Lower Albert Road, Central 🅣 2521 7251 🅦 www.hkfringeclub.com

### Cinemas
**Palace IFC Cinema** This 8-screen cinema complex in the IFC Mall has all the bells and whistles technology-wise, and is the most advanced in Hong Kong. 🅐 IFC Mall, 8 Finance Street, Central 🅣 2388 6268

**UA Pacific Place** Great sound system, comfy seats – one of the most comfortable choices for movie goers. 🅐 Pacific Place, 88 Queensway, Admiralty 🅣 2869 0322

**Windsor Cinema** A four-screen comfortable Cineplex just west of Victoria Park. 🅐 311 Gloucester Road, Causeway Bay 🅣 2388 3188

## Kowloon

Kowloon lies just north of Hong Kong Island, a Star Ferry ride across Victoria Harbour. Its hills create a dramatic backdrop for what has been called 'one of the world's best cityscapes'. Kowloon actually means 'nine dragons'. This refers to the eight hills around that represented the eight resident dragons; the ninth dragon was the Emperor.

The northern border of Kowloon is Boundary Street and this separates the district from the New Territories. The main Kowloon districts are Tsim Sha Tsui, Tsim Sha Tsui East, Yau Ma Tei and Mong Kok.

Tourists are usually most familiar with Tsim Sha Tsui because here you'll find the greatest concentration of hotels, restaurants and shops as well as such attractions as the Space Museum, Kowloon Park, a fine art museum and a new cultural centre. The area also has a lively nightlife and what's known as 'the golden mile of shopping'.

Tsim Sha Tsui East is built on reclaimed land dotted with shopping, entertainment and restaurant complexes, hotels and some good museums.

Yau Ma Tei has a very 'Chinese' feel about it and some interesting markets – including the jade market and the famous Temple Street Night Market. This is a good area to look for lower-priced hotels.

Mong Kok is mostly residential and industrial, but you'll find the Bird Market here, along with the Ladies' Market.

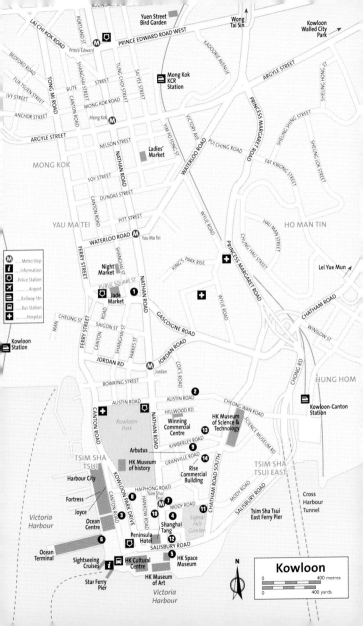

**Kowloon**

LAI CHI KOK ROAD
BEDFORD ROAD
FUK TSUEN STREET
IVY STREET
ANCHOR STREET
TONG MI ROAD
BOUNDARY STREET
PORTLAND ST
SHANGHAI STREET
BUTE STREET
CANTON ROAD
STREET
TUNG CHOI STREET
SAI YEE STREET
Yuen Street
Bird Garden
PRINCE EDWARD ROAD WEST
Prince Edward
Mong Kok
KCR Station
Mong Kok
KADOORIE AVENUE
ARGYLE STREET
PRINCESS MARGARET ROAD
SHEUNG HONG ST
Wong
Tai Sin
Kowloon
Walled City
Park

ARGYLE STREET
NELSON STREET
MONG KOK ROAD
Mong Kok
VICTORY AVE
YIM PO FONG ST
PUI CHING ROAD
WATERLOO ROAD
SHEUNG SHING STREET
SHEUNG LOK STREET
FAT KWONG STREET
HO MAN TIN
HAU WONG STREET
CHUNG HAU STREET

MONG KOK
Ladies'
Market
SOY STREET
DUNDAS STREET
CANTON ROAD
PITT STREET
NATHAN ROAD

YAU MA TEI
WATERLOO ROAD
Yau Ma Tei
FERRY STREET
SHANGHAI ST
KING'S PARK RISE
WYLIE ROAD
PRINCESS MARGARET ROAD
Lei Yue Mun

M ..... Metro Stop
i ..... Information
..... Police Station
..... Airport
..... Railway Stn
..... Bus Station
..... Hospital

Kowloon
Station

Night
Market
Jade Market
PUBLIC SQUARE ST
1
NATHAN ROAD
GASCOIGNE ROAD
WYLIE ROAD
CHATHAM ROAD

MAN ST
CHEONG ST
FERRY STREET
CANTON
SHANGHAI ST
SAIGON ST
PARKES ST
JORDAN RD
Jordan
COX'S ROAD
WINSLOW ST
CHONG RD
HUNG HOM

BOWRING STREET
AUSTIN ROAD
AUSTIN ROAD
2
CHEONG WAN ROAD
Kowloon-Canton
Station

CANTON ROAD
HILLWOOD RD
NATHAN ROAD
Winning
Commercial
Centre
HK Museum
of Science &
Technology
SCIENCE MUSEUM RD
13

Kowloon
Park
Arbutus
KIMBERLEY ROAD
GRANVILLE ROAD
9
14
Rise
Commercial
Building

TSIM SHA
TSUI
HK Museum
of history
CHATHAM ROAD SOUTH
TSIM SHA
TSUI EAST

Harbour City
Fortress
Joyce
KOWLOON PARK DRIVE
CANTON ROAD
HAIPHONG ROAD
Tsim Sha
Tsui
HANKOW ROAD
MODY ROAD
7
10
Shanghai
Tang
4
Signal
Hill
Garden
MODY ROAD
SALISBURY ROAD
Tsim Sha Tsui
East Ferry Pier
Cross
Harbour
Tunnel

Victoria
Harbour
Ocean
Centre
3
8
Peninsula
Hotel
12
11
5

Ocean
Terminal
Sightseeing
Cruises
i
HK Cultural
Centre
HK Space
Museum
N

Star Ferry
Pier
HK Museum
of Art
Victoria
Harbour

**Kowloon**

0          400 metres
0          400 yards

## SIGHTS & ATTRACTIONS

### Kowloon Park

Once an old 19th-century military base, the park has now become an all-in-one recreational venue. Along with the expected walks and trails, there's an open-air sculpture garden featuring local and overseas sculptors, an aviary, a hedge maze, a Chinese garden and a bird lake with flamingos and other waterfowl. For kids, there's a playground, three outdoor pools and an Olympic-size indoor pool. On Sunday afternoons there are free kung fu demonstrations.

**ⓘ** 2724 4522 **Ⓦ** www.lcsd.gov.hk

### Kowloon Walled City Park

This new park doesn't have all the attractions of other city parks. That said, it re-creates the style of a beautifully landscaped classical southern Chinese garden. Once a semi-lawless, high-rise slum, it was transformed into an award-winning park in 1995. You can wander by man-made hills and along winding paths to flower gardens and a sculpture garden filled with bonsai, bamboo and shrubs.

**ⓐ** Tung Tau Tsuen Road **ⓘ** 2716 9962 **Ⓦ** www.lcsd.gov.hk
**ⓛ** 06.30–23.00, admission is free

### Ladies' Market

This market in Mong Kok specialises in ladies' wear, but you can also find men's and children's clothing. Sizes tend to be on the small side. Accessories such as handbags, shoes, sunglasses, wigs, luggage and watches are also available.

**ⓐ** Tung Choi Street

## Lei Yue Mun

This charming old fishing village is rapidly modernising, but it still provides a chance to see something authentic before it disappears. You can take the MTR for an afternoon of wandering around the alleyways lined with hundreds of tanks filled with marine life. You can choose dinner from one of these, and the vendor will cook it for you.

ⓐ On the very southern tip of Kowloon in the eastern part of Victoria harbour

*Get your fortune told in the Temple Street Night Market*

**Temple Street Night Market**

Running from about 16.00 until 24.00, this is the liveliest night market in Hong Kong and definitely the place to haggle for a bargain. Set aside the whole evening for your trip to this market, and be prepared to be entertained. As well as shopping for cookware, clothing, sweaters, designer bags and sunglasses you can have your fortune told by palm readers or astrologers near the Tin Hau Temple. There are street singers who perform Cantonese opera as well as pop songs. What's more, the market is full of *dai pai dong* (food stalls) that specialise in seafood. Finally, it provides a wonderful people-watching opportunity.

**⒜** Temple Street

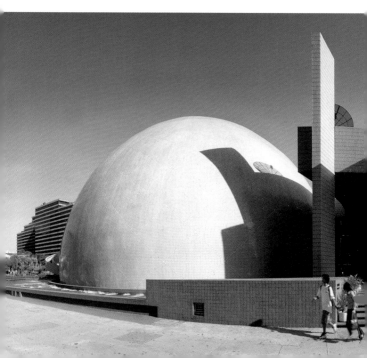

### Yuen Po Street Bird Garden

If you spot someone out on the street walking their bird, there's a good chance they bought it at the Bird Garden. The Chinese love birds and there are a multitude of them here squawking, chirping but most of all singing. People mill about buying and selling or simply just admiring the birds in their bamboo cages. It's a great place to take pictures and will provide you with a true Hong Kong experience.

ⓐ Main entrance facing Boundary Street and another entrance facing Yuen Po Street ⓦ www.lcsd.gov.hk ⓒ 07.00–20.00

⬤ *Let the Space Museum expand your horizons*

**THE SYMPHONY OF LIGHTS**

This is a spectacular nightly multimedia event and, according to *Guinness World Records*, is the world's largest permanent light and sound show. It involves more than 30 key buildings on both sides of Victoria Harbour, which are decked in lights that glow in myriad colours when a switch is flicked on.

🛈 The shows starts at 20.00 and runs for approximately 20 minutes. English narration is on the radio every night on 103.4 FM. ☎ 3566 5665 for more information

## CULTURE

### The Hong Kong Museum of Art

Five permanent galleries showcase a vast collection of ceramics, lacquer ware, jade, cloisonné, textile, wall hangings, scrolls and a great deal more. There are also many special exhibits. To make sure you have up-to-date information, it's best to check the museum's website.

ⓐ 10 Salisbury Road, Tsim Sha Tsui ☎ 2721 0116 ⓦ www.lcsd.gov.hk

### Hong Kong Space Museum

Kids love the interactive rides and exhibits along with a Hall of Astronomy and a whole load of information on space exploration. There's a Space Theatre as well, where OMNIMAX films (which provide a full multimedia experience) are shown.

ⓐ 10 Salisbury Road, Tsim Sha Tsui ☎ 2721 0226
ⓦ http://hk.space.museum

◯ *There aren't many cities where a bird will tell your fortune*

## Wong Tai Sin

A very popular Taoist temple, you can wander through halls dedicated to the Buddhist Goddess of Mercy and Confucius. Alternatively, you can throw numbered sticks out of a bamboo container and have your fortune read on the sticks selected. There's also a clinic that advises on both Western and Chinese herbal treatments.

ⓐ 2 Wong Tai Sin Estate ⓣ 2327 8141 ⓦ www.siksikyuen.org.hk

## RETAIL THERAPY

**Arbutus** A factory outlet where you can buy favourite brands of active wear and other hip sports clothing. 📍 29B Granville Road, Tsim Sha Tsui 🕐 11.00–23.00

**Fortress** If your hair dryer has conked out and you need assurance that the next one you buy is reliable, this chain of shops is the place to go. The friendly, helpful staff have a good stock of electrical and electronic goods, including cameras, stereos, CD players, plugs and so on. What's more the prices are low. 📍 Level 3, Harbour City, 5 Canton Road, Tsim Sha Tsui 📞 2116 1022

### LUCKY JADE & LOVELY PEARLS
Tagged as 'best buys' in Hong Kong, it's a good idea to scoop up a little information about pearls and jade before you set out to purchase. It might even be wise to check out how you can tell real from fake.

With the backing of the Hong Kong Tourism Board, gemmological experts Henry Cheng and Alex Chan hold free workshops every Tuesday and Thursday 09.30–11.00 at Hari's Bar, M/F, in the Holiday Inn. These knowledgeable experts explore the facts and myths about pearls and jade, their history, how they're graded and where to get the best quality for the best price.

**Holiday Inn** 📍 50 Nathan Road, Tsim Sha Tsui. 📞 2311 2532 to sign up for the classes

▶ *The Yau Yat Tsuen Festival Walk Shopping Centre in Kowloon*

**Harbour City** This is the largest shopping mall in Tsim Sha Tsui and it's easy to get lost, so pick up a map on your way into the mall. There are five interconnecting shopping arcades, including Ocean Terminal and Ocean Centre. ⓐ 5 Canton Road, Tsim Sha Tsui ⏱ 10.30–20.00

**Joyce** Looking for Prada? This is where you'll find it, along with other top brands, accessories and cosmetics. Joyce has several stores and is a Hong Kong institution. ⓐ 106 Canton Road, Tsim Sha Tsui ⏱ 12.00–22.30 Mon–Sat, 12.00–19.00 Sun

**Rise Commercial Building** Considered a current fashion hot spot, this mall is tucked away from view near the factory outlets in Granville Road. The lesser-known designers are located here, along with a henna tattoo parlour. ⓐ 5–11 Granville Circuit, Tsim Sha Tsui

**Shanghai Tang** The baby of an entrepreneur named David Tang, the main store is on HK Island, but it has spin-offs in New York and London. It sells clothes, fabrics and a host of objects 'made by Chinese' that are traditional Chinese with a twist. Among the usual leather coats, cheongsams and silk objects, you can also buy a Mao clock. ⓐ Intercontinental Hotel, Level 1, 18 Salisbury Road, Tsim Sha Tsui

**Winning Commercial Centre** Here in this off-the-beaten-track centre, young, trendy designers have local fashion labels, unusual imported fashion and second-hand clothing. ⓐ 46–48 Hillwood Road, Tsim Sha Tsui

## TAKING A BREAK

**Kubrick Bookshop Café £** ❶   If you have time to spare before catching a movie at the Cinematheque (where art-house films and re-runs are screened), you can browse through a good selection of film-related books and magazines while enjoying a coffee and sandwiches or pasta. ❷ 3 Public Square Street, Yau Ma Tei 🕒 11.30–22.00

**Kyushu-Ichiban £** ❷   Bargain priced sushi along with rice and noodle dishes – this makes a quick snack on a busy day. ❷ Ground and 1st floor, 144 Austin Road, Tsim Sha Tsui ☎ 2314 7889

**Main Street Deli £** ❸   For a quick New-York style deli lunch in between shopping bouts, you can get really serious 'deli' here: hot Reuben sandwiches, latkes, pizza, burgers and so on. The Deli's other contribution to Hong Kong life is the 'doggy bag'. ❷ Langham Hotel, 8 Peking Road, Tsim Sha Tsui ☎ 2375 1133

**Nathan's ££** ❹   For an incurable sweet tooth, Nathan's has 30-plus desserts every evening in a sumptuous dessert buffet. ❷ Hyatt Regency Hotel, 67 Nathan Road, Tsim Sha Tsui ☎ 2311 1234 🕒 20.00–23.00

**Peninsula Hotel Lobby ££** ❺   This is the city's most famous place for afternoon tea. Here you can nibble your cucumber sandwiches and scones as you listen to live classical music and watch an endless parade of fascinating people going by. ❷ Salisbury Road, Tsim Sha Tsui ☎ 2920 2888

**Ruby Tuesday ££** ❻ Visit this venue for a major heavy-duty salad bar and large portions for lunch, à la Americaine. ⓐ Shop Unit P26, Telford Plaza, Kowloon Bay ❶ 2376 3122

## AFTER DARK

### Restaurants

**Banana Leaf Curry House £** ❼ The formula here is: make good curry in lots of varieties and serve it with a gimmick – in this case, banana leaves for plates. Service is brisk and prices are reasonable. The place is always full and there are Malaysian, Indian and Thai curries from which to choose. ⓐ Golden Crown Court, 68 Nathan Road, Tsim Sha Tsui ❶ 2721 4821 ⓦ www.bananaleaf.com

**Fat Angelos £** ❽ The winning formula here is a cheerful ambience, huge servings plus complimentary salads and hot bread while you're waiting to dine. Main courses are the usual Italian fare – with pastas so huge two can dine on one serving. ⓐ Kowloon Centre, 35 Ashley Road, Tsim Sha Tsui ❶ 2730 4788

**Chang Won Korean Restaurant ££** ❾ In Little Korea, this is authentic Korean cuisine, *bulgogi* (popular beef dish) and all. ⓐ 1G Kimberley Street, Tsim Sha Tsui ❶ 2368 4606

**The Chinese ££** ❿ Cantonese food is served here in an intimate setting that echoes a 1920 Chinese teahouse. The restaurant moves away from the traditional red-and-gold décor and from traditional food presentation by presenting dishes in a way that

◐ *Nathan Road is the main thoroughfare in Kowloon*

Westerners might be more familiar with. ➌ In the Hyatt Regency, 67 Nathan Road, Tsim Sha Tsui ☎ 2311 1234

**Spring Deer ££** ⓫   This Peking-style eatery has been around for three decades and offers good food for reasonable prices. If your mouth is watering for honey-glazed Peking duck, this is a good place to try it. Excellent hot-and-sour soup, as well as other northern specialities. ➌ 42 Mody Road, Tsim Sha Tsui ☎ 2366 4012

**Felix £££** ⓬   This restaurant, which is at the top of the Peninsula Hotel, is avant-garde in its design to complement a creative Pacific Rim fusion menu. To savour the atmosphere without damaging your budget too much, the restaurant has an early-bird special (before 19.00) three-course prix-fixe dinner. ➌ Peninsula Hotel, Salisbury Road, Tsim Sha Tsui ☎ 2315 3188 ⓦ www.peninsula.com

**Fook Lam Moon £££** ⓭   For almost 50 years, Fook Lam Moon has been serving exotic dishes that are synonymous with Cantonese cuisine – abalone, bird's nest soup and shark's fin soup – as well as more classic Cantonese choices. A legion of fans claims no other restaurant in Hong Kong does Cantonese as well. ➌ 53–59 Kimberley Road, Tsim Sha Tsui ☎ 2366 0286 ⓦ www.fooklammoon-grp.com

### Bars & clubs
**Aqua Spirit** Brews with a view is all the rage in Hong Kong and this bar at the top of one of Kowloon's newest skyscrapers is getting rave reviews. ➌ 30th floor, 1 Peking Road, Tsim Sha Tsui ☎ 3427 2288

**Bahama Mama's** Wrapped in a kitschy Caribbean décor, this bar and dance club has great fruit cocktails and

dancing until 04.00. ❷ 4–5 Knutsford Terrace, Tsim Sha Tsui
❶ 2368 2121

**Felix** Perched on the top of the Peninsula Hotel, Felix has a view to
knock your socks off – just one reason why the chic crowd who
patronise the bar insist it's the city's finest venue for drinking.
Drinks are expensive, but the atmosphere is heady. ❷ 28th floor,
Peninsula Hotel, Salisbury Road, Tsim Sha Tsui ❶ 2366 6251
Ⓦ www.peninsula.com ❶ 18.00–02.00

**Lobby Lounge** Try one of the lounge's 'Nine Dragons' cocktail
as you take in the view of Victoria Harbour and Hong Kong
Island. Great spot to watch the Symphony of Lights laser show,
which takes place nightly for 20 minutes from 20.00. ❷ Hotel
Inter-Continental Hong Kong, 18 Salisbury Road, Tsim Sha Tsui
❶ 2721 1211

**Rick's Café** This typical Western-style bar and disco is a great
place to meet locals. It has an unpretentious atmosphere with
mainstream, pop and dance music which play all night.
❷ 53–55 Kimberley Road, Tsim Sha Tsui ❶ 2311 2255

**Performing arts**
**Hong Kong Cultural Centre** is the territory's premier arts venue and
home to both the Hong Kong Philharmonic Orchestra and the Hong
Kong Chinese Orchestra. Most of the opera and ballet is staged in a
2,100-seat Grand Theatre. There are other smaller concert halls. On
Thursday evenings and Saturday afternoons, free live performances
take place in the foyer and forecourt. ❷ 10 Salisbury Road, Tsim Sha
Tsui ❶ 2734 2009 Ⓦ www.hkculturalcentre.gov.hk

# New Territories

The New Territories extend from Boundary Street in Kowloon to the Shum Chun River and are a dramatically beautiful panorama of mountain ranges and valleys behind a rugged coastline.

While the New Territories and the outlying islands make up 90 per cent of Hong Kong's land mass, they have limited facilities compared to Kowloon and Hong Kong. Much of this large land area has been gobbled up for housing estates and industrial development, but enough park land still remains to make the New Territories excellent hiking terrain.

Since there have been small settlements and villages here for hundreds of years, it is possible to see remnants of life in days of yore on a day trip via bus or train.

◆ *Breathtaking hiking scenery*

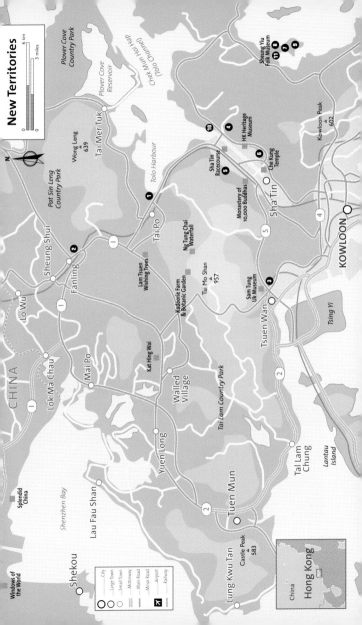

**RAIL TRAVEL IN THE NEW TERRITORIES**
ⓘ Use the following public transport systems to make your travel in the New Territories easier.

**Kowloon–Canton Railway (KCR)** Ⓦ www.info.gov.hk
**Light Rail Transit (LRT)** Ⓦ www.info.gov.hk
**Mass Transit Railway (MTR)** ⓘ 2881 8888 Ⓦ www.mtr.com.hk and www.info.gov.hk

ⓘ An Octopus card will make your rail journeys cheaper (see page 58 for fuller details) ⓘ 2266 2266
Ⓦ www.octopuscards.com

◗ In the New Territories you can catch a glimpse of old traditions

## SIGHTS & ATTRACTIONS

The best way to explore the New Territories is by the KCRC (railway). Pick up a copy of the booklet *Discover Hong Kong by Rail* from the Hong Kong Tourist Board.

### Che Kung Temple
This Taoist temple is dedicated to a Sung dynasty general who was deified for his devotion to the villagers of Tin Sam. The general suppressed a revolt in southern China and safeguarded villagers from the plague. Don't leave without turning one of the brass windmills in the courtyard for good luck.
ⓐ 7 Che Kung Miu Road, Tai Wai ☎ 2603 4049

### The Hong Kong Heritage Museum
With the exception perhaps of hiking the mountain trails, this is the best reason to come to the New Territories. It is one of Hong Kong's best museums and a 'must see' for anyone interested in the history and heritage of the region. The Heritage Hall is the best place to start. Displays document the changes in how people have lived throughout the centuries. There are ceramics, bronzes, art, furniture and wonderful pieces of jade. For kids, there's a toy museum and a hands-on discovery gallery.
ⓐ 1 Man Lam Road, Tai Wai ☎ 2180 8188 ⓦ www.heritagemuseum. gov.hk ⓛ Closed Tues; admission free on Wed

### Lam Tsuen Wishing Trees
In the village of Lam Tsuen, you can visit a group of giant banyan trees to burn joss sticks and incense papers to make your wishes come true.

### Lung Yeuk Tau Heritage Trail

The trail takes walkers through almost a dozen centuries-old villages, five of which are enclosed within stout walls for safety reasons. Most are connected with the Tang clan, one of the historic Five Great Clans of the New Territories.

ⓘ Information on the trail can be picked up at the Hong Kong Tourism Board's Visitor Information & Services Centres. The HKTB also has maps and a hiking/wildlife guidebook plus other recommended hikes on www.discoverhongkong.com

### Mai Po Wetlands

More than 300 species of birds have been recorded at Mai Po along with a number of Hong Kong's reptile and mammal species. Access to the wetlands is limited so if you would like a tour it's best to contact WWF Hong Kong in advance to find out about its guided public visits.

ⓣ 2526 4473 ⓦ www.wwf.org.hk

### The Monastery of 10,000 Buddhas

In Sha Tin, the temple sits at the top of a wooded hill accessed via a path lined with golden, scarlet-lipped Buddhas. It's a 400-step climb, but you will be rewarded by the sight of the tiny Buddha statues lining the walls (there's actually about 13,000), each one different. The temple was established by a monk named Yuet Kai, now embalmed, covered in gold leaf and placed in a glass case.

ⓦ www.10kbuddhas.org

▶ *An old man tends to the gods*

## Sam Tung Uk Museum

Until a few years ago, members of the Chan clan lived in this 18th-century village and carried on with their daily lives. When the last person left, it was turned into a museum. Four of the houses have been restored to their original condition and furnished with traditional Chinese furniture.

ⓐ 2 Kwu Uk Lane, Tsuen Wan ❶ 2411 2001
ⓦ http://hk.heritage.museum ❶ 09.00–17.00 Mon–Wed; admission free

## Sheung Yiu Folk Museum

This is a good glimpse into Hakka life in the remains of a fortified village built in the 19th century. You can see household goods and belongings along with farm equipment.

ⓐ Pak Tam Chung Nature Trail, Sai Kung ❶ 2792 6365
❶ 09.00–16.00, closed Tues

## RETAIL THERAPY

**New Town Plaza** Located in the Sha Tin, this is a huge shopping mall where the locals shop. Selling a mid-price range of goods of all types, it is well worth a visit but can be crowded at weekends.
ⓝ Accessible through the KCRC railway; change at Kowloon Tong Station if taking the MTR

**Tai Po Megamall** This is a group of shopping malls in the district which is less crowded than New Town and is easily accessible by KCR and KMB buses. ⓝ Take the KCR feeder bus K12 from Tai Po Market Railway Station

## TAKING A BREAK

Whether it's for lunch or dinner, here are some cheap and mid-range restaurants offering a variety of different foods.

**Chung Shing Thai Curry House £ ❶** This is part of a strip of restaurants, but judging by the popularity of this curry house, it may be the best. The curried crab is highly recommended. ⓐ 69 Tai Mei Tuk Village, Tin Kok Road, Tai Po ☏ 2664 5218 🕒 09.00–24.00

**Fung Ying Seen Koon £ ❷** After hiking the Lung Yeuk Tau Heritage Trail, this provides a vegetarian lunch at low cost with lots of imaginative dishes made from mushrooms and bean curd. ⓐ 66 Pak Wo Road, Fanling ☏ 2669 9186

**Gallo Café £ ❸** After the Sam Tung Uk Museum, this is a good place to sample free-range chicken, steamed and delivered whole to the table. Alternatively, try the honey-basted deep-fried eel on an outdoor covered pavilion. ⓐ 250 Sheung Cheung Wai, Tsuen Wan ☏ 2495 5555 🕒 07.00–24.00.

**Maxim's Palace Chinese Restaurant £ ❹** This is a large restaurant with the usual Cantonese dishes plus dim sum, seafood and barbecued Peking duck. ⓐ New Town Plaza, Sha Tin ☏ 2693 6918 🕒 07.30–23.45

**New Town Plaza £ ❺** For a quick snack in this area, try Oliver's Super Sandwiches.

**Royal Park Chinese Restaurant £** **❻** Cantonese food with good dim sum on the weekends ❷ Second floor, Royal Park Hotel, 8 Pak Hok Ting Street, Sha Tin ❶ 2601 2111

**Tung Kee Restaurant £** **❼** This is typical dining alfresco on the waterfront in Hong Kong with junks in the harbour and fishermen offering their catch. ❷ 96-102 Man Nin Street, Sai Kung ❶ 2792 7453 ❶ 11.00–23.00

**Anthony's Catch ££** **❽** A full-service Italian seafood restaurant with ultra-fresh fish served in huge portions and a great Sunday brunch that features such foreign delicacies as waffles with maple syrup. ❷ Ground floor, 1826B Po Tung Road, Sai Kung ❶ 2792 8474 ❿ www.anthonyscatch.com

**Chuen Kee Seafood Restaurant ££** **❾** There are a number of seafood restaurants to sample along the waterfront, but this is a good bet where you can select your dinner from a tank and then have it deliciously prepared. ❷ 51 Hoi Pong Street, Sai Kung Town ❶ 2791 1195

**Lung Wah Restaurant ££** **❿** This restaurant is straight out of a B-movie set and a little difficult to get to. It is famous for its roasted squab (pigeons), which are served with a side dish of greens with bamboo shoots and mushrooms and warm towels for your hands. ❷ 22 Ha Wo Che, Sha Tin ❶ 852 2691

◀ *There is also a modern urban side to the New Territories*

**Sauce ££** ⓫ Delicious European fare with outdoor seating. Good value. ⓐ 9 Sha Tsui Path, Sai Kung ⓐ 2791 2348 ⓦ www.sauce.com.hk

### Pubs & bars

**Cheers Sports Bar** As you might expect, this pub caters to the large expatriate population that lives in Sai Kung – especially when football and rugby are being show on the TV screens. Friendly atmosphere and open until the wee hours. ⓐ 28 Yi Chun Street, Sai Kung ⓣ 2791 6789

**Steamers** Another sports bar with a good selection of beers and wines plus a decent menu, not just pub stuff. ⓐ 18–32 Chan Man Street, Sai Kung ⓣ 2792 6991

**Tai Po Market** There are several pubs and country clubs along Kwong Fuk Road and the adjacent Luk Heung Lane, Tung Cheong Street. It is about a 5-minute walk from the Tai Po Market KCR Station. Overnight transport is readily available on Kwong Fuk Road to take you back to the downtown of Kowloon and Hong Kong.

---

🔘 *View over Cheung Chau and the Outer Islands*

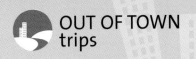

# OUT OF TOWN
trips

# The Outer Islands

For Hong Kongers, the Outer Islands mean escape from congested city life, plus a chance to dine on seafood by the seaside and frolic on the beaches. The three most favoured islands by visitors to Hong Kong are Cheung Chau, Lamma and Lantau. That said, there are a few others, each with a particular charm. Peng Chau, for example, is much smaller than 'the big three' and has a charming little village that sells a locally made pottery.

## GETTING THERE

Regular ferry services ply between Hong Kong and the Outer Islands leaving early in the morning and returning in the evening. The ferries are cheap, comfortable and usually air conditioned.

### FERRY SERVICES
- **New World First Ferry** ☎ 2131 8181 🅦 www.nwff.com.hk. Alternatively, go to its service centre at 🅐 Pier 6, the Outlying Islands ferry pier. Their ferries sail to Cheung Chau, Langtau and Peng Chau.
- The **Hong Kong and Kowloon Ferry** serves Lamma (☎ 2815 6063 🅦 www.hkkf.com.hk) and also has a customer service centre at 🅐 Pier 4, Outlying Islands ferry pier.
- If you are on a limited schedule, there are organised tours with **HKKF Travel** (☎ 2533 5339 🅔 info@hkkf.com.hk) to Cheung Chau and Lamma.
- **Watertours** (☎ 2926 3868 🅦 www.watertourshk.com) has a whole variety of tours including to the Outer Islands. The rides are generally from 35 to 50 minutes long.

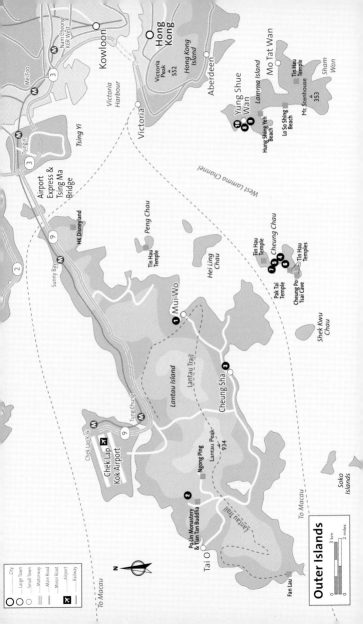

**Outer Islands**

To Macau

N

Kowloon

Nam Cheong/
KGK West

Mei Foo

3

M

Tsing Yi

M

3

Airport
Express &
Tsing Ma
Bridge

2

9

Sunny Bay

M

Chek Lap Kok

M

Tung Chung

9

Chek Lap
Kok Airport

Lantau Island

Lantau Trail

Ngong Ping

Lantau Peak
934

Po Lin Monastery
& Tian Tan Buddha ②

Lantau Trail

Tai O

Fan Lau

To Macau

HK Disneyland

Peng Chau

Tin Hau
Temple

Hei Ling
Chau

Mui Wo ①

Cheung Sha ③

Pak Tai
Temple

Cheung Chau
Tin Hau
Temple ⑦⑤⑥④
Cheung Po
Tsai Cave

Tin Hau
Temples

Shek Kwu
Chau

Soko
Islands

West Lamma Channel

Victoria Harbour

Victoria

Aberdeen

Hong
Kong

Hong Kong Island

Victoria Peak
552

Yung Shue
Wan ⑪⑩⑨⑧

Lamma Island

Hung Shing Yeh
Beach

Lo So Shing
Beach

Mo Tat Wan

Tin Hau
Temple

Mt Stenhouse
353

Sham
Wan

Key:
◯ City
◯ Large Town
○ Small Town
Motorway
Main Road
Minor Road
Railway
✈ Airport

0        3 km
0    2 miles

● Try to avoid taking ferries at weekends if you can, because they are busy and crowded with locals heading to the islands.

## LANTAU

This is Hong Kong's largest island and the first one visitors see, since they land here at the international airport. About 88,000 people live on Lantau compared to Hong Kong Island's 1.5 million – even though Lantau is twice as big. More than half the island is a designated park so there are excellent mountain trails including the 70-km (44-mile) Lantau Trail, which passes over Lantau and Sunset Peaks. The famous Tian Tan Buddha is here, plus Po Lin Monastery along with good beaches including Cheung Sha, the longest in Hong Kong.

## SIGHTS & ATTRACTIONS

### Tai O

One of the more interesting trips on the island is a visit to Tai O, a Tanka village on the west coast that used to be an important trading port with China. Today, it is a place where visitors come to ride a rope-tow ferry pulled mostly by elderly Hakka women, to walk around the village watching merchants processing salt fish or to visit some of the workshops of resident craftspeople. Traditional houses still stand in the centre of the village and you can get a glimpse of the seafaring past on the waterfront where some of the village's famous stilt houses still remain.

🚍 Take bus No 1 from Tung Chung, bus No 21 from Ngong Ping

---

● *The waterfront at Tai O*

## Fan Lau

Fan Lau Fort was built in 1729 to guard the channel from pirates and a nearby stone circle dates back to the Neolithic or Bronze Age. The only way to reach Fan Lau is on foot from Tai O.

Ⓝ Walk south from the bus station for 250 m (820 ft) then pick up stage No 7 of the coastal Lantau Trail for about 8 km (5 miles)

## Giant Tian Tan Buddha

Situated on the Ngong Ping plateau at an elevation of 738 m (about 2,400 ft), this Buddha is so huge you'll have your first glimpse of it while on the bus en route. Clocking in at more than 30 m (almost 1,000 ft) and weighing 250 tonnes, it's the world's largest seated outdoor bronze Buddha and can be seen from as far away as Macau on a clear day. Make sure you're fit because there are more than 260 steps up to the Buddha, but the climb is well worth it. It's a dramatic photo for shutter bugs.

Ⓝ From Silvermine Bay, take the No 2 bus bound for Ngong Ping and make sure you have the exact fare of HK$25 or use the handy Octopus card (see page 58). The ride from Silvermine Bay takes about 45 minutes

## Hong Kong Disneyland

What can you say about this attraction other than it's Fantasyland, Adventureland and Tomorrowland executed in a Chinese setting. The 126-ha (311-acre) theme park was opened in late 2005, so it is still a hot, new attraction for the locals. The park is linked by rail with the MTR at the new futuristic Sunny Bay station on the Tung Chung line.

Ⓝ Board the dedicated train for Disneyland Resort station and the theme park

**PINK ELEPHANTS ... NO, DOLPHINS!**

Think of a marine animal made of bubble gum and that's pretty much the colour of these Chinese white dolphins, which can be seen in the coastal waters off Lantau (if you're very lucky). Now threatened by environmental pollution, these once-abundant dolphins are down in numbers to between 100 and 200. There has been a lot of controversy about the whole situation, including protests that the natural coastline of Lantau Island was eroded during land reclamation and the construction of Hong Kong International Airport. Sewage dumping, over-fishing, chemical dumping and boat traffic all take their toll, not to mention fishing that often traps the dolphins in nets.

For more information and organised dolphin-watching cruises contact **Hong Kong Dolphin Watch** ❶ 2984 1414 ⓦ www.hkdolphinwatch.com

**Po Lin Monastery**

This huge Buddhist monastery and temple complex was built in 1924 and attracts many visitors both because of its location near the giant Buddha and also for its simple vegetarian restaurant – good, inexpensive and substantial food. Known as the Buddhist Kingdom in the South, the monastery ranks first for structure among the four most popular Buddhist temples in Hong Kong. After visiting the temple, if you want to see the sun rise on the Fong Wong Shan Mountain next morning, you can stay in the temple overnight.

ⓐ Ngong Ping, Po Lin ❶ 2985 5248

## TAKING A BREAK

Be it for lunch or dinner, here's a selection of restaurants that may appeal.

**Bahce £** ❶ A small restaurant serving Turkish food such as stuffed vine leaves and filo pastry filled with cheese plus the usual falafel and kebabs. ⓐ 3 Ngan Wan Road, Mui Wo Centre, Mui Wo (Silvermine Bay) 🕐 11.30–23.00

**Chinese Vegetarian Restaurant £** ❷ This is really just a huge dining hall at the Po Lin Monastery where you can pick and choose from a buffet of well-prepared vegetarian dishes which includes a lot of bean curd and mock-meat dishes. ⓐ Po Lin Monastery, Ngong Ping, Po Lin ☎ 2985 5248

**Stoep ££** ❸ A beautiful location right on the beach with food served alfresco. Barbecued meats cooked South Africa style are a speciality, but there are other continental dishes and a good wine list. ⓐ 32 Lower Cheung Sha Village ☎ 2980 2699/9465 🕐 10.00–22.00

## AFTER DARK

**China Beach Club** Pleasant rooftop bar and open-air balcony overlooking Silvermine Bay Beach. Good food. ⓐ 18 Tung Wan Tau Road ☎ 2983 8931 🕐 12.00–22.00, happy hour all day Thur–Sat

◀ *Goddesses surround the giant Tian Tan Buddha*

**China Bear** This is a good place to relax with a micro brew or one of a long list of good beers before leaving Lantau since it is close to the ferry pier and bus terminal. ⓐ Mui Wo Centre, Mui Wo ⓣ 2984 9720 ⓛ 10.00–02.00

## CHEUNG CHAU

At one time, the residents of Cheung Chau were full-time fishermen and part-time pirates who did a little smuggling on the side. The island, after all, was perfectly located to prey on passing ships. One of the more famous pirates, Cheung Po Tsai, made a base on the island and you can still visit the cave in which he allegedly stowed his booty.

The island has a few beaches and windsurfing is a highly popular pastime. It also proudly boasts that a native son won the gold medal in windsurfing in the 1996 Atlanta Olympics. Even though the island is only 2.5 sq km (about 270,000 sq ft) it supports a population of about 30,000, many of these commuters who work on Hong Kong Island or Kowloon.

## SIGHTS & ATTRACTIONS

### Beaches

There are a number of good beaches on the island but one of the best is Tung Wan on the eastern end of Tung Wan Road. It's a large beach by Hong Kong standards and a good, safe place to swim. Shark nets are up during the swimming season, which is May to October. Other beaches include those at Tai Kwai Wan and Tung Wan Tsai on the northern end.

**Cheung Po Tsai Cave**

On the southwestern peninsula, this cave is allegedly the favourite hiding place of the notorious pirate Cheung Po Tsai. It is a 2 km (just over 1 mile) walk from Cheung Chau village along Sai Wan Road. The pirate, who once commanded a flotilla of 600 junks and had a private army of 4,000 men, surrendered to the Qing government in 1810 and became a bureaucrat. Rumour insists that his treasure still lies buried somewhere on the island.

## CULTURE

**Tin Hau Temples**

Since Tin Hau was the empress of heaven and the patroness of seafarers, it's not surprising that there are four temples on the island dedicated to this deity.

- The Pak She Tin Hau Temple is about 100 m (330 ft) northwest of the Pak Tai Temple.
- Nam Tan Wan Tin Hau Temple is just north of Morning beach.
- Tai Shek Hau Tin Hau Temple is to the west of Sai Wan Road.
- Sai Wan Tin Hau Temple is west of Western Bay.

**The Pak Tai Temple**

This is the oldest and most famous temple on the island and dates back to 1783. Guarded by two stone lions, it is dedicated to the Taoist deity Pak Tai whom legend says spared the island's residents from the plague when it was decimating other islands in the area. As the god of the sea, Pak Tai protects fishermen. Inside, there's an iron sword measuring 1.5 m (5 ft) in length that was found by local fishermen and thought to be 1,000 years old. However, the temple

is most famous as the focus point of the annual Cheung Chau Bun Festival and inside the temple is a sedan chair in which Pak Tai's statue is carried during the Festival (see page 10).

## TAKING A BREAK

Here are some places for light refreshments, lunch or dinner.

**Bayview Coffee Shop £** ❹   For a simple lunch, this coffee shop located on the beach in the Warwick Hotel has an enclosed terrace. Serves sandwiches, dim sum and other Chinese dishes. ⓐ Warwick Hotel, Tung Wan Beach ☎ 2981 0081 ⌚ 11.30–14.30

**Hometown Teahouse £** ❺   After a day on Tung Wan Beach, this relaxed place with a terrace run by a likeable Japanese couple is perfect for lunch or dinner. They also serve afternoon tea, Japanese style, which means sushi, pancake and tea. ⓐ 12 Tung Wan Road ☎ 2981 5038 ⌚ 12.00–24.00

**Hong Kee ££** ❻   Along with a number of other restaurants, Hong Kee is famous for its lobster with black bean sauce. ⓐ Ground floor, 11A Pak She Praya Road ☎ 2981 9916 ⌚ 10.30–22.30

**New Baccarat Seafood Restaurant ££** ❼   One of the oldest of the many restaurants crowding the waterfront, it has seating under a canopy and specialises in seafood. ⓐ 9A Pak She Praya Street ☎ 2981 0606 ⌚ 11.00–22.30

---

▶ *The Bun Festival offers such spectacles as floating children!*

## Bars & pubs

**Lai Kam's** This is a Cheung Chau institution and is named after the owner, although it's also known as the Patio Café. As an open-air café with a pub, it's attached to the Windsurfing Centre at Tung Wan Beach. ⓐ Cheung Chau Windsurfing Water Sports Centre, 1 Hak Pai Road ⓣ 2981 8316 ⓛ 12.00–19.00

**Morocco's Bar & Restaurant** On the waterfront, this was a favourite drinking spot when there was a large expatriate community living on Cheung Chau. It's still a good place to have a beer and enjoy some decent Indian food. ⓐ 117 Praya Street ⓣ 2986 9767 ⓛ 10.00–03.00

## LAMMA

As the closest of the Outer Islands (about 25 to 35 minutes by ordinary and fast ferry), Lamma is also Hong Kong's third-largest island with a population of about 12,000.

It's still largely undeveloped with no cars on the island but a great place for hiking on a 1½-hour Family Trail that links the island's two villages.

The hike has some great ocean views as well as glimpses of Ocean Park and Aberdeen on Hong Kong Island.

The smaller of the two villages, Sok Kwu Wan, is the place to go for alfresco seafood. The larger, Yung Shue Wan, has a population of young bohemian foreign residents, which is its big draw. The island also has some good beaches, including Lo So Shing Beach, the most beautiful on the island.

If planning a day visit to Lamma, take the ferry to Sok Kwu Wan and stop to enjoy a delicious seafood lunch before hiking to a nearby beach. From there you can take the trail to Yung Shue Wan for dinner before heading back to Central. Ferry services are more frequent to this town than Sok Kwu Wan.

## SIGHTS & ATTRACTIONS

### Beaches

**Hung Shing Yeh Beach** is Lamma's most popular beach but to avoid the crowds try to come during the week. There are toilets and changing rooms and shark nets to protect bathers.

**Lo So Shing Beach** is south of Hung Shing Yeh and below a Chinese Pavilion on the path. While not big, this is the most beautiful beach on the island and it does have trees for shade.

**Mo Tat Wan** is a clean and relatively uncrowded beach but has no lifeguards.

**Sham Wan** is another beautiful bay, and is considered the best and most secluded beach. To get here, you have to follow a narrow overgrown track. This is the only beach in Hong Kong where green turtles still lay their eggs in the nesting season (June–October) and the beach is closed then.

### The Kamikaze Caves

On the eastern shore, these caves were constructed by the occupying Japanese forces during World War II and were designed to hide small speedboats packed with explosives that would be used in suicide attacks on Allied shipping. The war ended before they could be used and the caves have since been allowed to deteriorate and be reclaimed by nature.

**Mount Stenhouse**

For climbers, this 353-m (1,158-ft) high mountain has spectacular views from the summit over all of Lamma and beyond to Hong Kong Island and Lantau. The route up is a tough scramble on a rocky path but worth the struggle.

## TAKING A BREAK

**The Blue Bird £** ❽ An unadorned little spot with basic but tasty Japanese dishes and good sushi and sashimi. ⓐ 24 Main Street, Yung Shue Wan ⓣ 2982 0687 ⓛ 11.30–15.00 & 17.30–00.30

**The Bookworm Café £** ❾ Basic food, but everything is vegetarian and organic (try the fruit juices and organic wine). Best of all, it's downright inexpensive. It has it's name because there's a second-hand bookshop here as well as an Internet café.
ⓐ 79 Main Street, Yung Shue Wan ⓣ 2982 4838 ⓛ 10.00–21.00

**Sampan Seafood Restaurant ££ ❿** This restaurant is popular with locals for seafood and pigeon dishes, as well as dim sum. ⓐ 16 Main Street, Yung Shue Wan ❶ 2982 2388 ● 06.00–22.30

### Pubs

**The Deli-Lamma** In keeping with its hip name, this place with its terrace on the harbour caters to a hip crowd in the evening. There's on-tap cider and basic pub fare. ⓐ 36 Main Street, Yung Shue Wan ❶ 2982 1583 ● 09.00–late

**Diesel Sports Bar** A favourite hangout of the expat community, this place is crammed full on Saturday nights with cheering football and rugby fans. ⓐ 51 Main Street, Yung Shue Wan ❶ 2982 4116 ● 18.00–late

● *The tranquility of Lamma*

# Further afield

## MACAU

Much was made of the political handover of Hong Kong in 1997 to China after more than 150 years of British rule, but Macau was a Portuguese colony for 450 years before it was returned to Chinese hands. As the first and last major European colony in Asia, little wonder that it remains one of the most hybrid places on Earth culturally swinging back and forth between Chinese and Portuguese.

Everywhere you look you can see a fusion of Asian and Mediterranean, whether it's in the architecture, churches, food, temperaments or lifestyle.

Pastel-coloured churches sit on cobblestone streets which are identified on blue-and-white *azulejos* (Portuguese enamel tiles) near Buddhist and Taoist temples. In town, Chinese stores are jumbled with colonial-style buildings, and shopkeepers blend Chinese practicality with Portuguese warmth and flair.

A day trip or an overnight stay in Macau are appealing for a number of reasons: there seems to be something for everyone here.

There are temples, gardens, fortresses, beaches, excellent museums, historical treasures and casinos for the gambling-addicted. Hotels tend to be cheaper and, as a duty-free port with lots of new, smart boutiques, Macau is a mecca for shopping.

## GETTING THERE

Macau lies 65 km (40 miles) to the west of Hong Kong and is easy to reach by ferry, jetfoil or catamaran.

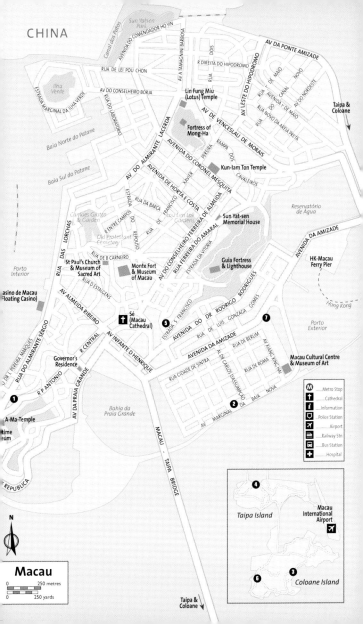

CHINA

Sun Yatsen Park

Canal dos Patos

AVENIDA DO COMENDADOR HO YIN

AV DA PONTE AMIZADE

RUA DE LEI POU CHON

RUA DIREITA DO HIPODROMO

AV A TAMAGNINI BARBOSA

RUA DOIS

DE MAIO

NOVO

AV DO NORESTE

AV LESTE DO HIPODROMO

Ilha Verde

ESTRADA MARGINAL DA ILHA VERDE

AV DO CONSELHEIRO BORJA

RUA DO LABORATORIO

Lin Fung Miu (Lotus) Temple

Fortress of Mong-Ha

RUA DO CANAL

AVENIDA 7 DE MAIO

RUA NOVO DA AREIA PRETA

Taipa & Coaloane

Baia Norte do Patane

AVENIDA DO CORONEL MESQUITA

AV DE VENCESLAU DE MORAIS

PEREIRA

RAMPA DOIS

Kun-Iam Ton Temple

CAVALEIROS

Baia Sul do Patane

AV DO ALMIRANTE LACERDA

AVENIDA DE HORTA E COSTA

XAVIER

RUA DA BARCA

RUA DE FRANCISCO

Reservatório de Água

ESTRADA DE REPOUSO

RUA DE FRANCISCO ROU LUN LOK Gardens

Sun Yat-sen Memorial House

Camões Grotto & Garden

RUA D ENTRE CAMPOS

RUA DAS LORCHAS

Old Protestant Cemetery

RUA DE B CARNEIRO

St Paul's Church & Museum of Sacred Art

Monte Fort & Museum of Macau

AV DO CONSELHEIRO FERREIRA DE ALMEIDA

RUA FERREIRA DO AMARAL

ESTRADA DA VITORIA

Guia Fortress & Lighthouse

AVENIDA DA AMIZADE

HK-Macau Ferry Pier

Porto Interior

RUA D ESTAGENS

RODRIGUES

Hong Kong

asino de Macau (Floating Casino)

AV DO ALMEIDA RIBEIRO

Sé (Macau Cathedral)

ESTRADA S FRANCISCO

AVENIDA DO DR RODRIGO RODRIGUES

LUIS GONZAGA GOMES

RUA DE

⑤

⑦

Porto Exterior

Governor's Residence

R CENTRAL

AV DA PRAIA GRANDE

AV INFANTE D HENRIQUE

AVENIDA DA AMIZADE

RUA DE BERLIM

RUA DE ROMA

AV YANG CHI TAI

Macau Cultural Centre & Museum of Art

RUA DR L PEREIRA MARQUES

RUA DO ALMIRANTE SERGIO

R P ANTONIO

RUA CIDADE DE SINTRA

RUA DE CARLOS D ASSUMPCÃO

RUA DA BAIA NOVA

①

A-Ma-Temple

time eum

Bahia da Praia Grande

②

AV MARGINAL DA BAIA

REPUBLICA

MACAU - TAIPA BRIDGE

N

Macau

0        250 metres
0        250 yards

Ⓜ ......Metro Stop
✝ ......Cathedral
ⓘ ......Information
🚓 ...Police Station
✈ ......Airport
🚆 ....Railway Stn
🚌 ....Bus Station
✚ ......Hospital

④

Taipa Island

Macau International Airport

③ Coloane Island

⑥

Taipa & Coloane

Taipa & Coloane

Since Macau peninsula is only 1.5 km (1 mile) wide and 4.75 km
(3 miles) long, you can walk to most of the sights. However, there
are taxis (painted black and beige) that are inexpensive.

## SIGHTS & ATTRACTIONS

### Camoes Grotto & Garden
He likely didn't live in Macau, but Portugal's famous 16th-century
poet Luis Vaz de Camoes has always been much loved here.
Locals convinced that Camoes made the journey to the East say
that he composed one of his most famous works here, *The Lusiads*.
A bust of the poet sits in the garden.
ⓐ Praca Luis de Camoes ⓒ 06.00–23.30

### Lou Lim Lok Garden
A wealthy 19th-century Chinese merchant enchanted with the
famous gardens in Suzhou, China, created this replica for his own
and posterity's pleasure. There are narrow winding paths, a zig-zag
bridge to deter bad spirits, carp pools, rock grottos and bamboo

▶ *The Lou Lim Lok Garden*

groves. A peaceful place, even more so in the morning when local tai chi practitioners are going through their exercises and bird lovers, with their birds, fill the garden with song.

ⓐ Estrada de Adolfo Loureiro ⓣ 853 356622 ⓛ 06.00–18.00

## Monte Fort

For history buffs, the Monte Fort overlooking St Paul's was built by the Jesuits in the early 17th century and is the site of the city's most famous battle in 1622. At the time the fort was guarded by a small force of African slaves, soldier and priests, one of whom fired a lucky shot that landed in the powder supply of the invading Dutch ships and drove them back. From this point you'll find a great view of most of Macau on a clear day.

ⓐ Monte Fort ⓦ www.macautourism.gov.mo ⓛ 10.00–18.00

## Old Protestant Cemetery

This restored cemetery has some interesting 19th-century graves of European and American Protestants who lived in Macau.

ⓐ Camoes Garden, Praca Luis Camoes ⓛ 06.00–23.30

## St Paul's Church

On a visit here, photo buffs invariably head to St Paul's Church following the mosaic tiles from Macau's main colonial-era square to the striking ornate façade of the church, all that remains of the once-powerful cathedral. Originally built in 1602, the church caught fire during a typhoon in 1835 and burned to the ground. Walking up the grand staircase leading to the façade you can understand why historians call this the finest monument to Christianity in Asia.

ⓐ Rua do Belchior Carneiro

### Sun Yat-sen Memorial House

Sun Yat-sen is widely recognised by Chinese people everywhere as being the modern founder of their country. This was once the home of Dr Sun Yat-sen's first wife and it contains a collection of flags, photos and other memorabilia.

ⓐ Avenida Sidonio Pais ☎ 574 064 ⏰ 10.00–17.00, admission free

ⓘ There are a number of special things to do in Macau like trying your luck at the horse or dog races. Alternatively, you can people-watch at the 24-hour-a-day floating casino. Try taking an evening stroll along Macau's Fisherman's Wharf to browse through souvenir shops, the amusement park and man-made volcano. Then end your day watching the sun set from Macau's own 'space needle'.

## CULTURE

### Macau Museum of Art

A small museum displaying historical paintings, contemporary local artists, Chinese calligraphy, pottery and so on.

ⓐ Avenida Xian Xing Hai ☎ 853 7919814 ⓦ www.artmuseum.gov.mo
⏰ 10.00–18.30, closed Mon

### Museum of Macau

This museum in the ancient Monte Fort has an excellent overview of Macau's history, its traditions and its art. Displays include paintings and photos showing Macau through the centuries, a peek at its architecture and cuisine, and a comparison of the Chinese and European civilisations at the time of their encounter in the 16th century. There are interesting comparisons between the two writing systems of the cultures, their philosophies and

religions. A re-created street scene lined with colonial and Chinese shop façades is well done.

**2** Citadel of Sao Paulo do Monte **1** 853 357911

## Temple of Kun Iam Tong

Dedicated to the Goddess of Mercy, this is one of the most important temples in Macau and is well worth a visit. The temple was founded in the 13th century, but most of its buildings date from 1627. A statue of Kun Iam, who is dressed like a bride, is attended by 18 golden figures on the walls that represent the 18 wise men of China. In the same room you'll see an odd statue with bulging eyes that is supposed to represent Marco Polo. In the garden behind the temple, there are four intertwined banyan trees known as Lovers' Trees because they symbolise marital fidelity. Local legend says that they grew from the graves of two lovers who committed suicide.

**a** Avenida do Coronel Mesquita **(** 07.00–18.00

## RETAIL THERAPY

Things tend to be cheaper here than in Hong Kong, so while the choices may not be as plentiful, the prices are better. The most popular purchases seem to be curios, furniture and antiques.

**(** There are many dealers who will claim that the item they are trying to sell you is authentically antique. But it may not be. Reproductions from China are everywhere. Some of the more reputable shops can be found on Rua de Sao Paulo.

**(** *The grand staircase and façade of St Paul's Church*

Knitwear is another popular buy in Macau, since the territory manufactures woollen and cotton garments. If you shop around, you can pick up seconds, discontinued lines or overruns of popular labels for a song.

Electrical goods, gold jewellery, Chinese herbs and medicine are also popular.

> **SPECIAL TREATS**
> Soak up a bit of art history with rotating shows in a gallery called the Leal Senado. Or do a little shopping along the Avenida do Infante Dom Henrique or the Avenida de Almeida Ribeiro, the main shopping areas. Antiques on Rua de Sao Paulo, Rua de Sao Antonio and Rua das Estalagens are especially good, as well as collector item stamps at the main post office.

## TAKING A BREAK

One of the best reasons to visit Macau is for a taste of the subtle blending of Chinese and Portuguese flavours known as Macanese cuisine. Being world explorers, the Portuguese brought spices from Africa, codfish and vegetables from Europe, chilis from India, and sweet potatoes, kidney beans and peanuts from Brazil. These are used in a dish called *feijoada* – a stew of pork, black beans, cabbage and spicy sausage that is washed down with a young wine called *vinho verde*. Here are some great places to eat, day or night.

**Antica Trattoria da Isa £** ❶  In the nightlife district, this restaurant is always crowded but its 18 different kinds of pizza are great as well as other traditional Italian dishes. ⓐ Edificio Vista Magnifica Court 40–46, Avenida Sir Anders Ljungstedt ⓣ 755 102

**A Lorcha ££** ❷ Some of the best Portuguese food in Macau, the dishes to sample here are *piri piri, feijoada* and *porco balichao tamarino*. ⓐ 289A Rua do Almirante Sergio ⓣ 313 193

**Fernando's ££** ❸ This brick building on the beach with a pavilion happens to be *the* place to dine if you like beach dining. The menu is strictly Portuguese with Fernando, the owner, doing wonderful things with codfish, chicken, pork ribs, suckling pig, prawns, mussels and so on. They bake their own bread and stock only Portuguese wine. ⓐ Praia de Hac Sa 9 Coloane Island ⓣ 882 531

**Flamingo ££** ❹ For the best foray into Macanese cuisine, try Flamingo with its hot flamingo-pink walls and terrace dining. The specialities of the house are a unique blend of Chinese, Portuguese, African, Indian and Malay to create the delicious Macanese taste. ⓐ Hyatt Regency Hotel, Taipa Island ⓣ 831 234 ⓦ www.macau.hyatt.com

**Clube Militar de Macau ££–£££** ❺ For a special night out, this is excellent Macanese/Portuguese cuisine in an atmospheric setting. For lunch, there's a first-class buffet complemented by the best wine list in town. ⓐ Avenida da Praia Garande 795 ⓣ 714 009

**Espaco Lisboa £££** ❻ This tiny two-storey restaurant is known for its traditional, country-style Portuguese food with mouth-watering fried codfish cakes, sautéed clams in garlic and coriander and Portuguese cabbage soup just for starters. One of the best finds

in Coloane Village. ⓐ Rua das Gaivotas 8, Coloane Village, Coloane Island ❶ 882 226

**Naam £££** ❼ The décor is great, the food is sublime – everything you'd expect from a Mandarin Hotel. ❸ Ground floor, Mandarin Oriental Hotel, 956–110 Avenida da Amizade ❶ 793 4818

## AFTER DARK

❶ For nightlife, remember that Macau was once the sin centre for Asia with opium dens and lots of intrigue. Things have certainly changed but it's wise to avoid the tacky floorshows and hostess clubs, and to check with Macau Tourism for recommendations. Macau Fisherman's Wharf is a safe bet and there are trendy discos on Avenida do Infante D Henrique.

### Pubs & clubs
There are pubs and clubs in great abundance in Macau, especially in the NAPE, an area of reclaimed land. Theme bars line the waterfront and some have live music.

> **DELICIOUS TREATS**
> To sample the special Macanese blending of these two cultures, the **Nga Tim Café** (❶ 853 882086) on the main square of Coloane Village is an inexpensive but delicious place for lunch. While in the village (and after trying Coloane's two beaches), a couple of good dining spots are **Espaco Lisboa** (❶ 853 882226) for gourmet Portuguese and **Fernando's** (❶ 853 882264) for moderately priced Portuguese seafood dishes served on a patio on the beach.

**Casablanca Café** This is an elegant spot with cool jazz in the background and photos of Hollywood and Hong Kong film stars decorating the walls. ⊘ Vista Magnifica Court Building, Avenida Doutor Sun Yat-sen, Macau Peninsula ⊘ 751 281

**Embassy Bar** A live band and a small dance floor that fills up as the night wears on. Probably the classiest watering hole in Macau. ⊘ Mandarin Oriental Hotel, 956–110 Avenida da Amizade ⊘ 567 888

⬤ *Macau's food traditions are quite different to Hong Kong's*

**Signal Café** A very popular spot with young locals in the waterfront area. ⓐ Avenida Dr Sun Yat-sen ⓣ 751 052

**Performing arts**
**The Macau Cultural Centre** is the city's main venue for classical music concerts, dance performances and studio film screenings.
ⓐ Avenida Xian Xing Hai ⓣ 555 555 ⓦ www.ccm.gov.mo/en/intro.htm

The Macau Government Tourist Office also publishes a free monthly guide – *Macau Travel Talk* – that lists what's going on. It is available at most large hotels and MGTO offices.

## ACCOMMODATION

For overnight stays, there are a few hotels and resorts from the expensive **Hyatt Regency Macau** (ⓐ 2 Estrada Almirante Marques Esparteiro, Taipa Island ⓣ 853 831234 ⓦ www.macau.hyatt.com) to the moderately priced **Pousade de Coloane**, a small, family owned property on a hill above Cheoc Van Beach (ⓐ Praia de Cheoc Van, Coloane Island ⓣ 853 882144).

### SPECIAL ECONOMIC ZONES
Special Economic Zones (SEZs) were developed by the People's Republic of China to encourage foreign investment in China, bring much-needed jobs, technical knowledge and future tax revenues in return for significant tax concessions at start-up. They are not unlike SEZs in other parts of the world and currently include cities in the provinces of Guangdong, Fujian, Hainan, Hunchun and Pudong (Shanghai).

## SHENZHEN

Shenzhen, the Special Economic Zone that straddles the Hong Kong border to the north, is China's richest city and was one the People's Republic of China's five original SEZs.

Fewer than 30 years ago, it was a little town with a population of 20,000. Today, its population exceeds 4 million and it has a kind of boomtown aura. (For location see map on page 51.)

Shenzhen has its own stock exchange, traffic congestion and skyscrapers sitting cheek by jowl. It also has pollution. But most of all it beckons to anyone wanting an even better bargain than they find in Hong Kong. Come here to have clothing made, shop for real bargains, have a massage or manicure, or just get a glimpse into where China is going without going to Beijing. Shenzhen is touted these days as China's most cosmopolitan city, so no matter where you go you will hear dialects and accents from all over the country. While most people come here to shop, there are a few other things to do, as listed on pages 135–6.

## GETTING THERE

From Hong Kong, you'll find buses run by a host of companies that leave from various points at different times during the day. Two companies to check out are: **CTS Express Coach** (☎ 2365 0118) and **Eternal East Cross Border Coach** (☎ 3412 6677 ⓦ www.eebus.com).

The most comfortable way to go is via KCR East Rail from East Tsim Sha Tsui station. Trains leave from around 05.30 to 24.00. From TST station to the border takes about 40 minutes.

ⓘ You will need a visa to enter Shenzhen. This is available either at the border or in Hong Kong (see page 140). Getting it at the border limits you to 5–7 days within the confines of Shenzhen SEZ. It's

recommended that you pay the extra and get a proper Chinese visa that will allow you to visit other places in China and also avoid a horrendous queue at the border.

## SIGHTS & ATTRACTIONS

### China Folk Culture Village

This village showcases China's 55 ethnic groups, their architecture, customs and traditions. You'll also find 24 life-size villages.
❶ 0755 2660 0626

### Splendid China

This is a theme park with miniatures of China's most historic buildings and sites, including the Temple of Confucius, the Great Wall of China and the Imperial Palace.
❶ 6600 626

### Shenzhen Sea World

About 30 km (19 miles) from the centre of the city, this attraction has aquatic performances that range from synchronised swimming to dancing with sharks. You'll find lots of aquariums filled with creatures from the sea.
ⓐ Xiaomeisha Recreation Centre, Yantian District ❶ 755 2506
ⓦ www.shenzhenwindow.net

### Window of the World

Taking a global look, the world's most famous monuments are here squeezed into 480,000 sq m (0.2 sq miles). The 108-m (354-ft) tall

◀ *Traditional Chinese embroidery*

Eiffel Tower dominates the skyline, and the sight of the Pyramids
and the Taj Mahal all in such close proximity are all part of the
slightly kitsch appeal of this theme park. Additionally, there's a
wide selection of international restaurants and mini exhibitions
on famous figures from world history. Window of the World allows
you to eat Mexican Food, see the Niagara Falls, then wander around
Angkor Wat. The site takes at least half a day to explore and every
day ends with a firework and laser show.

ⓐ Shijie Zhichuang ⓣ 755 2690

## RETAIL THERAPY

Shopping is the *raison d'etre* behind most day visits to Shenzhen
because prices for quality goods are lower than in Hong Kong and
bargainers can drive a harder bargain – sometimes reducing the
price by as much as 50 per cent.

**Lowu Commercial City** is a huge mall with 1,500 small shops that
offer more variety in goods than anywhere else in Shenzhen. Here
you can find a tailor to make a custom garment, then head up to
the Fabric Mall on the fifth floor for a custom-made suit or dress.
Each floor of the centre has a selection of shoe and handbag shops.
On the second floor, stalls sell freshwater pearls, jade, beads and
semi-precious stones.

**Hua Qiang Bei Lu** This is one of the newer shopping areas in
the heart of the city with rows and rows of small shops similar
to Lowu Commercial City.

ⓞ *See the world at Window of the World*

## TAKING A BREAK

Whatever time of day, here are some places to eat and drink.

**Noodle King £** If there's little time left over after running from shop to shop, this is a good stop for a quick lunch of dumplings, noodles and vegetable dishes. ⓐ 3021 Renmin Nanlu ⓣ 0755 8222 2348

**Ocean King Restaurant ££–£££** The best place in Shenzhen for seafood – always popular and packed. ⓐ Haishang Huang Jiujia, lll6 Jianshe Lu ⓣ 0755 8223 9000

### Bars & pubs
**Henry J Bean's Bar & Grill** Located in the Shangri-La Hotel, this is a comfortable and stylish place for an after-shopping drink. ⓣ 0755 8233 0888

ⓞ *Traditional ways persist in China's richest city*

## THE REST OF CHINA

China is such a vast country with so much to see that an 'extension' after a Hong Kong trip can only be a taste of what another trip could offer. Try to decide what appeals to you most – a cultural or historical experience, shopping, seeing the most famous sights or an adventure.

For culture, Yunnan and Sichuan introduce the many minority ethnic groups with their special customs and costumes.

For history, there's Xian with its amazing warriors or the fabulous bronzes of Sanxingdui.

Shanghai can't be beaten as a shopping experience, with Beijing close behind, adding as a bonus The Great Wall.

For an adventure, there are caravans to the vast northwestern deserts or the highest train ride in the world to the Tibetan plateau.

❶ All China trips require a visa. Obtaining one of these can take from one to three days. You'll need two photos, which you can get at one of the photo booths in the MTR.

❷ Visa Office of the People's Republic of China, 7th floor, Lower Block, China Resources Centre, 26 Harbour Road, Wan Chai.

▶ *Learning is fun at the Science Museum*

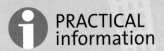

# PRACTICAL information

# Directory

## GETTING THERE
### By air
As the major gateway to China, Southeast Asia and much of the East, more than 70 international airlines operate between Hong Kong International Airport and 130 other destinations worldwide.

From the UK, the major airlines flying direct to Hong Kong without stopping en route are as follows.

**British Airways** ❶ 0845 773 3377 Ⓦ www.ba.com
**Cathay Pacific** ❶ 020 8834 8888 Ⓦ www.cathaypacific.com
**Qantas** ❶ 08457 747 767 Ⓦ qantas.co.uk
**Virgin Atlantic** ❶ 0129 345 0150 Ⓦ www.virgin.com/atlantic

## INTERNAL TRAVEL TO MACAU
### By ferry & helicopter
From Hong Kong to Macau, most people take the ferry, although the East Asia Airlines helicopter shuttle is becoming increasingly popular.

**New World First Ferry** (❶ 727 676 Ⓦ www.nwff.com.hk) has high-speed catamarans from Tsim Sha Tsui five times a day on weekdays with departures on the half-hour from 07.00. At weekends there are 33 daily departures. The trip takes between 65 and 75 minutes and tickets start at HK$140.

**TurboJet** (❶ 790 7039 Ⓦ www.turbojet.com.hk) has regular crossings that take between 55 and 65 minutes from Hong Kong to the ferry terminal in Macau.

---

❶ *The Mid-Autumn festival is one of Hong Kong's most important festivals*

**East Asia Airlines** (📞 727 288 🌐 www.helihongkong.com) has a helicopter shuttle from the helipad on top of the ferry terminal. The flight takes 16 minutes between HK and Macau.

## ENTRY FORMALITIES

Citizens of the UK, Republic of Ireland, other EU countries, the USA, Canada, Australia, New Zealand and South Africa must hold a valid passport extending at least six months after your planned departure date from Hong Kong. Nationals of most countries do not need visas for visits of up to 180 days.

## MONEY

The Hong Kong dollar (HK$) is made up of 100 cents. Coins are: bronze-coloured 10 cents, 20 cents and 50 cents; silver HK$1, HK$2 and HK$5; nickel and bronze HK$10. Denominations of notes are: HK$10, HK$20, HK$50, HK$500 and HK$1,000.

As a major financial centre, Hong Kong has no currency controls, which means you can bring in or send out as much money as you want. When changing money, banks usually offer the best rates, although the major banks levy a commission. The city has many

### CUSTOMS

Hong Kong may be a duty-free port, but there are certain items on which duty (and high duty!) is charged – for example, alcohol (100 per cent on spirits, 80 per cent on wine and 40 per cent on beer). You can bring in duty free 200 cigarettes and 1 litre of alcohol. Apart from this most things are permitted with the exception of firecrackers and fireworks and, of course, drugs.

licensed moneychangers such as Chequepoint (especially in the tourist areas) and while these are open at convenient hours (for example, Sundays, late in the evening) they offer less attractive exchange rates than the banks. ATMs can be found almost everywhere and are linked to most international money systems such as Plus, Cirrus and Maestro. The most widely accepted credit cards are Visa, MasterCard, American Express, Diners Club and JCB. Although the credit card companies forbid it, some shops may try to add a surcharge for credit cards.

ℹ When signing credit card receipts make sure you always write 'HK' in front of the dollar sign if it's not already there.

## HEALTH, SAFETY & CRIME

As with most Asian countries, the major risk for travellers are stomach upsets caused by eating contaminated fruit or vegetables, or drinking contaminated water. Drink only bottled water (where you can see that the seal has not been broken) or water that has been boiled for at least three minutes. Stay away from ice, raw food, unpasteurised milk and milk products, and raw shellfish, which has been linked to hepatitis outbreaks.

For its size, Hong Kong is a remarkably safe city but stick to well-lit areas if walking around at night. Police officers patrol frequently, especially in the Tsim Sha Tsui area, and they are helpful to visitors. To avoid hassles, exercise the usual common sense safety rules such as locking up your valuables in a safe, keeping an eye on belongings in crowded areas and being wary of people offering gambling or investment opportunities.

Hong Kong has world-class hospitals providing outstanding care, but the service is expensive so travel insurance is vital. In the case of an emergency, an ambulance will take you to a government-run public hospital where you will have to pay a large sum for emergency services. Treatment is guaranteed, so even if you can't pay immediately you can be billed later.

## OPENING HOURS

Generally, business hours are weekdays 09.00–17.00 and Saturdays 09.00–13.00. Major banks are open weekdays 09.00–16.30 and Saturdays 09.00–12.20. They are closed Sundays and public holidays.

The vast majority of shops are open every day 10.00–19.00. Stores in busy retail areas like Wan Chai, Causeway Bay and Tsim Sha Tsui stay open as late as 21.30. Museums are usually open six days a week 09.00–17.00 with one day closed (usually Monday or Tuesday).

## TOILETS

In the past, Hong Kong has been annoyingly short of public toilets but this is rapidly changing. New ones are being built and old ones upgraded with baby changing tables in both men's and women's toilets and good facilities for the disabled.

It's usually free to use these toilets, but keep tissues on hand because toilet paper quickly runs out. Restrooms in hotels and restaurants are usually the best bet as far as cleanliness goes.

## CHILDREN

Adults may find Hong Kong a shopper's paradise, but kids are not forgotten when it comes to attractions. Here are some of the top things for the younger set.

- **Yuen Po Street Bird Garden** Located on Yuen Po Street, this garden has various courtyards filled with trees and stalls selling

birds, cages and lots of non-caged birds swooping around.
ⓐ Main entrance facing Boundary Street and another entrance
facing Yuen Po Street ⓦ www.lcsd.gov.hk ⓛ 07.00–20.00

- **Central Escalator** Free, and great fun, this is the longest
  escalator in the world. It consists of three moving walkways
  and 20 elevated escalators, and was built as an unusual but
  practical form of transport for residents living in the upper
  levels. It's an interesting 20-minute experience, and you can
  get on and off to check out great shops and restaurants along
  the way.

- **Disneyland Theme Park** To the north of Discovery Bay, this new
  park has all the old favourites – Fantasyland, Adventureland and
  Tomorrowland plus more.
  ⓦ www.hongkongdisneyland.com

- **Ocean Park** This old favourite has a cable-car ride, Dragon
  rollercoaster and the stomach-churning Abyss turbo prop ride,
  plus marine animal shows and much more.
  ⓦ www.oceanpark.co.hk

- **Hong Kong Heritage Museum** Just southwest of Sha Tin
  town centre, this museum looks like an ancestral hall.
  As well as its large collection of arts it has a wonderful
  Children's Discovery Gallery. Here kids can peek into Hong
  Kong life or check out the Cantonese Opera Heritage Hall
  where they can make themselves up as Cantonese opera
  characters on a computer.
  ⓦ www.heritagemuseum.gov.hk

- **Hong Kong Space Museum and Theatre** Located on Salisbury Road, this venue has one of the largest planetariums in the world, a Space Theatre with IMAX films plus treasures such as a rocket-ship model, NASA's 1962 Mercury space capsule and Moon rocks.
  Ⓦ www.lcsd.gov.hk

- **Sampan tour** A 30-minute-long sampan tour of the harbour can be booked from Aberdeen Promenade.

❶ For more information, download HKTB's *Hong Kong Family Fun Guide* at www.discoverhongkong.com. Most of the admission fees and transport services are half-price for kids under 12 years of age.

## COMMUNICATIONS
### Phones
Hong Kong uses an 8-digit system and provides clear-sounding connections. The country code is 852. To get an English-speaking operator for directory assistance, dial 1081. Phone rates are cheaper from 21.00 to 08.00 on weekdays and throughout the weekend. If the phone you are using has the facility, dial 0060 first and then the number – rates will be cheaper at any time.

Public pay phones cost HK$1 for five minutes. Phones accept HK$1, HK$2, HK$5 and HK$10 coins. All local calls from private phones are free, but hotels will charge between HK$3 and HK$5 for local calls. Hong Kong has the world's highest per capita usage of cell phones, and they work everywhere, including tunnels!

## Post

With its British roots, the Hong Kong postal service is excellent – with letters often being delivered the same day they are sent in the city. International air mail is divided into two zones: Zone 1 includes China, Japan, Taiwan, South Korea, SE Asia and Indonesia; Zone 2 is everywhere else. Air mail generally takes from 3 to 8 days. Rates start at HK$2.50 (under 20 grams) for Zone 1 and HK$4.50 for Zone 2. Local mail is HK$1.40 for up to 30 grams. Aerogrammes are a uniform HK$2.30.

**General Post Office** (on Hong Kong Island) ⓐ 2 Connaught Place, Central District ⓒ 08.00–18.00 Mon–Sat, 09.00–14.00 Sun

### LONG DISTANCE CALLS

From Hong Kong, you can dial international direct dial calls from most public telephones with a phone card (Hello or Smartcards). These are available from 7-Eleven and Circle K convenience stores, Mannings pharmacies, Wellcome supermarkets, PCCW branches and retail outlets.

To place a call to someone outside Hong Kong, dial 001, then the country code, the local area code and the number. When dialling Hong Kong from abroad, drop the initial 0 from the local area code.

### Some country codes

| | |
|---|---|
| Australia (61) | Macau (853) |
| Canada (1) | Netherlands (31) |
| China (Mainland) (86) | New Zealand (31) |
| France (33) | South Africa (27) |
| Germany (49) | United Kingdom (44) |
| Japan (81) | United States (1) |

**Tsim Sha Tsui Post Office** (Kowloon) ❷ Ground Floor, Hermes House, 10 Middle Road 🕒 08.00–18.00 Mon–Sat, 09.00–14.00 Sun

ⓘ Postal boxes are lavender with lime-green posts, all clearly marked in English. Staff at the post offices speak English and there is Saturday delivery.

### COURIER SERVICES

For speedier delivery, letters and small parcels can be sent via **Speedpost** (ⓦ www.hongkongpost.com) to about 216 destinations worldwide within four days. These packages are automatically registered.

Other couriers are also available.
**DHL** ⓦ www.dhl.com
**Federal Express** ⓦ www.fedex.com
**UPS** ⓦ www.ups.com

### ELECTRICITY

Electrical current is 220 volts, 50 cycles alternating current (AC). Plugs can be confusing, though. While most take the British three square pins, some will take three large round prongs and others three small pins. Inexpensive plug adaptors are available in many stores and supermarkets.

ⓘ For overseas dual voltage appliances, be sure to bring a converter and an adaptor. Since Hong Kong is known for being high tech, blackouts and other electrical catastrophes are generally not a problem.

## TRAVELLERS WITH DISABILITIES

Because of its geography, Hong Kong is not the easiest city in the world for people with disabilities. Rail and underground stations have stairs, footpaths tend to be narrow and crowded, and there are many steep hills. Newer venues such as the City Hall, airport and Hong Kong Arts Centre *do* have facilities for wheelchairs and most have lifts with Braille panels. Wheelchairs can also negotiate the lower decks of most ferries and some buses are wheelchair accessible.

The huge airport has moving walkways as well as ramps, lifts and elevators. There are no special taxis for the disabled, but drivers do carry walking aids such as wheelchairs and crutches.

For more information on services for disabled travellers, contact:

**Joint Council for the Physically and Mentally Disabled**

Ⓦ www.hkcss.org.hk

**Hong Kong Sports Association for the Physically Disabled**

Ⓦ www.hksap.org

## FURTHER INFORMATION

### Hong Kong Tourism Board

The HKTB bends over backwards to be helpful, has a large willing staff and heaps of literature. The office hotline is open 08.00–18.00 to solve all problems.

Ⓘ 2508 1234 Ⓦ www.discoverhongkong.com

### HKTB Visitor Information & Service Centres

These are on Hong Kong Island, in Kowloon, in the International Airport on Lantau and in Lo Wu on the border with mainland China. In other parts of Hong Kong iCyberlink screens are

available from which you can access the HKTB website and
database 24 hours a day.
**Visitor's hotline** ☎ 2508 1234

**Hong Kong International Airport** @ Halls B on arrival level and
in the E2 transfers area 🕓 07.00–23.00
**Kowloon HKTB Centre** @ Star Ferry Concourse, Tsim Sha Tsui
🕓 08.00–20.00
**Hong Kong Island HKTB Centre** @ 99 Queen's Road, Causeway Bay
MTR station, near exit F 🕓 08.00–20.00
**Lo Wu HKTB Centre** @ 2nd floor, arrivals hall, Ko Wu Terminal
Building 🕓 08.00–18.00

**Free publications**
*HKTB Visitor's Kit* gives a description of the city's main tourist
attractions and information on shopping.

*Hong Kong Museums & Heritage* has information on how to reach
the city's museums and attractions using public transportation.

*Hong Kong maps* including bus and train maps.

**Useful websites**
**bc magazine** for nightlife and entertainment
Ⓦ www.bcmagazine.net
**HK Clubbing** Ⓦ www.hkclubbing.com
**Hong Kong Information Services Department** Ⓦ www.lcsd.gov.hk
**Hong Kong Yellow Pages** Ⓦ www.yp.com.hk
**South China Morning Post** Ⓦ www.scmp.com.hk

**FURTHER READING**

*East and West: The Last Governor of Hong Kong on Power, Freedom and the Future* by Chris Patten. The politician who oversaw the handover of Hong Kong writes about his experiences in the colony.

*Hong Kong: China's New Colony* by Stephen Vines. Hong Kong's story continues with a hard factual examination of the change in the territory after the British leave.

*Hong Kong: Epilogue to an Empire* by Jan Morris. The Welsh travel writer alternates chapters on Hong Kong's history with descriptions of its geography, economy, politics and society.

*Hong Kong: Portraits of Power* by Evelyn Huang. This looks at Hong Kong and China through the eyes of its most influential people – the elite of power, mystery and wealth such as Anson Chan, Dr Stanley Ho (the Casino King of Macau) and Li Ka Shing (in the top 20 of the world's wealthiest individuals). Photos by Lord Snowdon.

*Tai Pan* and *Noble House* by James Clavell. These two massive pieces of historical fiction trace the history of Hong Kong from 1841 in the wake of the Opium War to the present. In telling the story of Dirk Struan and his 'noble house' the books capture the spirit of the Western trading companies through their trials and tribulations.

*Traveler's Tales Hong Kong* by James O'Reilly. These 52 tales written by Pico Iyer, Paul Theroux and others range from cuisine to superstition and racism to race horses in the quest to discover the character of Hong Kong.

# Useful phrases

Hong Kong has two official languages, Cantonese and English. Cantonese is closely related to Mandarin Chinese and is spoken by more than 70 million people worldwide. It's a difficult language for English-speakers to learn: not only are words written in symbols but the same word can have different meanings depending upon the 'tone' (or pitch) in which it is spoken. Don't panic! You'll get by perfectly well with English but if you fancy trying a bit of Cantonese, here are some useful words and phrases with an approximate English pronunciation.

| English | Approx. pronunciation |
|---|---|
| **BASICS** | |
| Yes | h<u>ai</u> |
| No | ǹg•h<u>ai</u> |
| Please ... | ǹg•gòy ... |
| Thank you (very much) | dàw•j<u>e</u> (l<u>á</u>y) |
| Sorry | deui•ǹg•jew |
| I wish you well | lày hó |
| My name is ... | ng<u>á</u>w giu ... |
| Hello | hàa•ló |
| Hi | hày |
| Good morning | jó•s<u>à</u>n |
| Good afternoon | ńg•ngàwn |
| Good evening | m<u>á</u>an•ngàwn |
| I'm lost | ng<u>á</u>w d<u>a</u>wng•sàk•l<u>o</u> |
| Where are the toilets? | chi•sáw hái bìn•d<u>o</u> |
| Do you speak English? | l<u>á</u>y sìk•ǹg•sìk gáwng yìng•mán aa |
| I don't speak Cantonese | ng<u>á</u>w ǹg sìk gáwng gwáwng•dùng wáa |
| Do you accept | l<u>á</u>y•d<u>a</u>y sàu•ǹg•sàu ... aa |
|    credit cards? | seun•y<u>u</u>ng•kàat |
|    debit cards? | t<u>à</u>i•fún•kàat |
|    traveller's cheques? | léui•h<u>à</u>ng jì•piu |

| English | Approx. pronunciation |
|---|---|

## SHOPPING

| | |
|---|---|
| How much is it? | *gáy•dàw chín* |
| Can you write down the price? | *ng̀•gòy sé dài gaw gaa•chín* |
| That's too expensive | *taai gwai laa* |
| My size is ... | *ngáw jeuk ... ho̱* |
| Can I try it on? | *háw•ng̀•háw•yí si há̱a* |

## EATING OUT

| | |
|---|---|
| Breakfast | *jó•chàan* |
| Lunch | *ng̀•chàan* |
| Dinner | *má̱an•fa̱an* |
| Snack | *li̱ng•si̱k* |
| Excuse me! | *ng̀•gòy* |
| I'd like the menu | *ngáw séung yiu choy•dàan* |
| I'll have that | *ngáw dím lày máy* |
| I'm a vegetarian | *ngáw ha̱i si̱k jàai ge* |
| I'd like the bill please | *ng̀•gòy ngáw yiu má̱ai•dàan* |

## EMERGENCIES

| | |
|---|---|
| Help! | *gau•me̱ng* |
| Stop! | *ká̱y há̱i•do̱* |
| Thief! | *yá̱u cháat aa* |
| Fire! | *fó•jùk aa* |
| Call the police! | *faai•dì giu gíng•chaat* |
| Call an ambulance! | *faai•dì giu gau•sèung•chè* |

## NUMBERS

| | | | |
|---|---|---|---|
| One | *yàt* | Nine | *gáu* |
| Two | *yi̱* | Ten | *sa̱p* |
| Three | *sàam* | Eleven | *sa̱p•yàt* |
| Four | *say* | Twelve | *sa̱p•yi̱* |
| Five | *ńg̱* | Twenty | *yi̱•sa̱p* |
| Six | *lu̱k* | Fifty | *ńg̱•sa̱p* |
| Seven | *chàt* | One hundred | *yàt•baak* |
| Eight | *baat* | | |

# Emergencies

## EMERGENCY NUMBERS

❶ Emergency numbers are free.

**Ambulance/fire/police** ❶ 999
**Complaints against the police** ❶ 2574 4220
**Lost credit cards** American Express ❶ 2811 6122; Diners Club ❶ 2860 1888; MasterCard ❶ 8009 6677; Visa ❶ contact issuing bank in HK
**Lost passports** Contact your consulate after notifying the police at ❶ 2860 2000

## MEDICAL EMERGENCIES

**The Hospital Authority One-Stop Enquiry Service** has two 24-hour hotlines (❶ 2882 4866 and 2300 6555) that provide information on accident and emergency services, hospital fees, help with complaints, hospital phone numbers, locations and transport information.

The full range of accident and emergency services are provided 24 hours a day at the hospitals listed below.

**Prince of Wales Hospital** ⓐ 30–32 Ngan Shing Street, Sha Tin, New Territories ❶ 2632 2211

**Matilda Hospital** ⓐ 41 Mt Kellett Road, The Peak, Hong Kong ❶ 2849 0123

**Queen Mary Hospital** @ 102 Pok Fu Lam Road, Hong Kong Island
🕿 2855 3111

**Queen Elizabeth Hospital** @ 30 Gascoigne Road, Kowloon
🕿 2958 8888

## CONSULATES & EMBASSIES
Hong Kong is well represented for most countries; for a complete
list of consulates and embassies check the Hong Kong Yellow Pages.

**Australian** Consulate @ 23rd floor, Harbour Centre, 25 Harbour Road,
Wan Chai 🕿 2827 8881
**Canadian** Consulate @ 11th–14th floors, Tower One, Exchange
Square, 8 Connaught Place, Central 🕿 2810 4321
**New Zealand** Consulate @ Room 6508, 65th floor, Central Plaza,
18 Harbour Road, Wan Chai 🕿 2877 4488
**South Africa** Consulate @ Room 2706–2710, 27th floor, Great Eagle
Centre, 23 Harbour Road, Wan Chai 🕿 2577 3279
**UK** Consulate @ 1 Supreme Court Road, Central 🕿 2901 3000
**US** Consulate General @ 26 Garden Road, Central 🕿 2841 2211

The publishers would like to thank the following for supplying the copyright photos for this book: pages 12 & 31 Hong Kong Tourist Board; pages 123, 126, 131 Macau Government Tourist Office; pages 137 & 138 Panos; page 134 Pictures Colour Library; page 39 Rasmus Engell-Kofoed; page 85 Robert Harding World Imagery; all the remaining photos are from Helena Zukowski

Copy editor: Sandra Stafford
Proofreader: Lynn Bresler

### Send your thoughts to
# books@thomascook.com

- Found a great bar, club, shop or must-see sight that we don't feature?

- Like to tip us off about any information that needs updating?

- Want to tell us what you love about this handy little guidebook and more importantly how we can make it even handier?

Then here's your chance to tell all! Send us ideas, discoveries and recommendations today and then look out for your valuable input in the next edition of this title. As an extra 'thank you' from Thomas Cook Publishing, you'll be automatically entered into our exciting monthly prize draw.

Send an email to the above address (stating the book's title) or write to: CitySpots Project Editor, Thomas Cook Publishing, PO Box 227, The Thomas Cook Business Park, Unit 18, Coningsby Road, Peterborough PE3 8SB, UK.